THE
PRINCIPLES OF R.

AS PROFESSED BY

The Society of Christians,

USUALLY CALLED

QUAKERS;

*Written for the Instruction of their YOUTH,
and for the Information of STRANGERS.*

———

By HENRY TUKE.

———

THE SEVENTH EDITION, CORRECTED.

—◄◄◄◊►►►—

York:

PRINTED FOR W. ALEXANDER, AND SOLD BY HIM;
SOLD ALSO BY
DARTON, HARVEY, AND CO., AND W. PHILLIPS,
LONDON;
AND M. M. AND E. WEBB, BRISTOL.

1819.

Printed by HARGROVE, GAWTHORP, & COBB,
Herald-Office, Pavement, York.

INTRODUCTION.

CONSIDERING the many publications which already exist, explanatory of the Principles of our Religious Society, it may seem, to some persons, superfluous to publish any thing further on this subject. I have, notwithstanding, been long apprehensive, that a work is still wanting, which shall include the whole, or the most material part of our principles ; and, in a concise, yet perspicuous manner, convey a sufficient explanation and defence of them. The ample and excellent Apology of Robert Barclay, is too diffuse for the generality of young readers ; and it requires a more close and patient attention than many are willing to bestow. It would, however, in my apprehension, amply repay that attention : and I am so far from being desirous to lessen its use, that I wish particularly to recommend it to those of our society, who desire (what all should desire) thoroughly to understand, their own religious principles. If the language is not modern, it is still correct and clear ; if the work is thought too controversial, we should recollect, that the controversy is on subjects, the right understanding of which, is intimately connected with our existence as a Religious Society.

The light and miscellaneous reading of the present day, it is to be feared, disinclines many amongst us, as well as others, from subjects which require close attention and serious consideration; and I wish it may not also be a means, of weakening the attachment of many, to those religious truths, in which our highest duty and our deepest interest consist.

In this work, I have been desirous of inculcating the general principles of religion, and of Christianity, as well as those which are peculiar to our society; believing, that we can no longer exist, with any degree of consistency, than while those principles are maintained, which constitute the basis of the Christian Religion. These I consider, to be, faith in God, and a belief of the immortality of the soul; a humbling sense of the depravity of human nature, and of the necessity and benefits of a Redeemer; that this Redeemer is Christ Jesus our Lord; that what the Evangelists and Apostles have written concerning Him, is true, both in relation to his humanity and his Divinity, as are likewise their accounts of his many mighty works and miracles; his having, through the eternal Spirit, offered himself unto God for us, as a propitiation for our sins; and sent the Comforter, even the Spirit of Truth, to convince the world of sin, of righteousness, and of judgment; and to guide into all truth.

In treating of the Holy Scriptures, I have particularly endeavoured to obviate the principal objections made against them ; since it is by attempting to invalidate their authenticity and Divine authority, that the enemies of the Christian religion attack our faith. I have introduced the subject of the Scriptures, previously to the Chapter on the Christian religion; considering, that if the authenticity and veracity, to say nothing of the Divine authority, of these writings be established, it is then necessary only to show, what Christianity is, according to the Scriptures : a few arguments are, however, added, in support of the Christian Religion.

With respect to those principles which are peculiar to our Religious Society, I hope that, however singular they may appear to some, they will, on close examination, be found consistent with the nature and spirit, of the gospel dispensation. The conviction of this consistency has been increased on my mind, by the investigation which the writing of this work has occasioned; and, I trust, we are able to give such reasons for our dissent from other Christians, as may, at least, excuse it to those from whom we differ.

Although very little is quoted in this work from any books, but those of the Holy Scriptures, it may be proper

A 3

to say, that I am indebted to the writings of others, for many of the arguments which I have advanced. At a time when so much has been written, and well written, on these subjects, it is not to be expected, that many fresh arguments can be brought forward. Some new matter will, nevertheless, be found. The principal object aimed at in this work is, to digest what has been produced by reading and reflection, and to deliver it in such a manner, as may briefly, yet clearly, convey the sentiments designed to be inculcated. How far this object has been attained, is not for me to determine.

I wish not, by any thing which I have written, to promote a spirit of controversy. On the contrary, I desire the increase of that mutual charity, which it is alike our duty and our interest to cherish. To speak what we apprehend to be truth, is, however, sometimes necessary; and always so, if we speak at all. If we do this, as we ought to do, in love; and if what we say is received in the same spirit, we may be the means of stirring up the pure mind in each other; and of promoting our "growing up in Him, in all things, who is the Head, even Christ."*

* Ephesians iv. 15.

CONTENTS.

—

CHAP. I.

ON RELIGION IN GENERAL.

—

CHAP. II.

ON THE HOLY SCRIPTURES.

CHAP. III.

ON THE CHRISTIAN RELIGION.

CHAP. IV.

ON THE INFLUENCES OF THE HOLY SPIRIT.

CHAP. V.

ON DIVINE WORSHIP AND GOSPEL MINISTRY.

CHAP. VI.

ON BAPTISM AND THE SUPPER.

CHAP. VII.

ON THE RELIGIOUS OBSERVANCE OF DAYS AND TIMES.

CHAP. VIII.

ON OATHS AND WAR.

CHAP. IX.

ON AMUSEMENTS.

CHAP X.

ON DRESS AND ADDRESS.

CHAP. XI.

ON CIVIL GOVERNMENT.

CHAP. XII.

ON DISCIPLINE.

CHAP. XIII.

CHAPTER I.

ON RELIGION IN GENERAL.

Universal Importance of Religion.—The Belief of God its first Principle.—The next that of the Immortality of the Soul.—Universality of these Principles.—Arguments for them.—Faith their best support.

RELIGION is a subject which involves so much, both of the duty and interest of mankind, that there is no situation in life, which can exempt from the considerations and obligations it imposes on all men; or render superfluous those sources of enjoyment and consolation which it affords, to its true and humble possessors.

The first principle of religion is, the belief of a Supreme Being, distinguished by the name of GOD; a being, who is the Original Creator of all things; who hath all power in his hands; who is perfect in wisdom and knowledge; who is just and equal in all his ways; and whose tender mercies are over all his works. He knoweth our most secret actions, words, and thoughts ; for there is nothing hid from Him, with whom we have to do.

The next principle of religion, is the belief of the immortality of the soul, and of a future state of rewards and punishments, in which the great distinction will be made between the righteous and the wicked ; those inequalities which appear in this probationary state will be removed ; and a recompence given to every man according to his works.

Although these principles of religion are not attended with that kind of 'evidence, which the objects of our external senses generally afford ; yet it is not a little remarkable, that there are scarcely any other subjects, which have obtained such general belief and persuasion amongst mankind, though often mixed with many gross ideas. They are principles so interwoven with our natures, that it seems to indicate an extraordinary debasement, or perversion of mind, not to entertain truths so universally felt and acknowledged. They are, however, principles which may be supported by arguments, drawn from the nature of things ; and, notwithstanding the general consent to them, it may be proper to bring forward a few of these arguments.

The existence of a Supreme Being, the Creator of heaven and earth, is evident from the works of creation. The magnificence of some of these works ; the regularity and order with which they move in their appointed stations ; the beauty and use attendant upon others, with the important purposes which are accomplished by them, particularly to the animal creation, evince so clearly both design and power, as to afford an insuperable argument in favour of a Great First Cause, perfect in wisdom and goodness, as well as unlimited in power. To these considerations may be added, the wonderful arrangement of the animal economy. The different parts adapted to their different purposes with peculiar exactness and advantage, might well induce the pious Psalmist, to address his Maker in this emphatic language : "I will praise thee, for I am fearfully and wonderfully made ; marvellous are thy works, and that my soul knoweth right well."* Thus also a consideration of the other works of creation, in-

* Psalm cxxxix. 14.

duced the same Psalmist to celebrate his Maker's praise: "The Heavens declare the glory of God, and the firmament showeth his handy work. Day unto day uttereth speech, and night unto night showeth knowledge. There is no speech nor language where their voice is not heard.*" And again: "O Lord! how manifold are thy works; in wisdom hast thou made them all."†

Nor are we without arguments for our immortality, and a future state of retribution, the belief of which is, as it were, the soul of religion: for when we have entertained suitable ideas of a Supreme Being; when we feel those aspirations unto Him, and those desires to unite with Him, which frequently arise in our hearts; and particularly when we look at the state of the righteous and the wicked in this world; we have sufficient reason to conclude, that there is a part in man which is immortal: and that there must be a future state, in which virtue and vice will

* Psalm xix. 1, 2, 3.

† Psalm civ. 24. If any person should think it irregular, to bring forward passages from the Scriptures, before their authority has been proved; it may be observed, that these passages are not advanced as arguments, but as elucidations, in the same manner as any other writing might be quoted.

meet with their respective rewards, in a more signal manner than they appear to receive them in this life; thus showing that God is just and equal in all his ways, and righteous in all his thoughts.

But, notwithstanding these and other arguments, which might be adduced in support of those two first principles of religion, the soul seems most fully to rest upon and enjoy them, when they are felt as objects of faith, rather than of reason. They then become like self-evident truths, for which our own feelings are the best support, and which act in concert with that declaration: " Without faith it is impossible to please Him; for he that cometh to God must believe that He is; and that He is a rewarder of them that diligently seek him."* And we ought ever to remember, after all our reasonings on these subjects, that " Life and immortality are brought to light by the gospel."†

* Heb. xi. 6.   † 2 Tim. i. 10.

CHAP. II.

ON THE HOLY SCRIPTURES.

Nature and Design of the Scriptures.—Their claim to our regard and to the belief of their being divinely inspired—Objections answered—first to their Genuineness and Truth—next to their Inspiration.—All related of good men not intended for imitation.—Impartiality of the Scriptures.—Great judgment necessary in applying them.—Possibility of placing too much dependance on them.—On calling them the Word of God.

THESE writings are divided into two parts, the Old and the New Testaments. They commence with an account of the Creation of the world, and contain a history of more than four thousand years. Their object appears to be, to exhibit the various dispensations of God to mankind; to manifest many of his general and particular acts of Providence; to show the good effects of religion and virtue; and to set forth the lamentable evils, which are the consequence of walking in the paths of irreligion and profaneness. For the prevention of these evils, the Scriptures inculcate those principles of piety and morality, which contribute to the happiness of mankind, both here and hereafter; and there is not any general duty, religious or moral, in which they do not afford instruction and direction.

The Scriptures also contain many remarkable predictions concerning nations and individuals, with several prophecies of the coming of the Messiah, and of the dispensation of the gospel. Ancient history, both sacred and profane, gives account of circumstances, which show the fulfilling of many of these predictions; and the New Testament particularly relates the completion of those, which are given concerning "Him, of whom Moses in the law and the prophets did write."*

When we consider who were the writers of these volumes; what are the subjects, and what appear to be the objects of them; they claim, at first view, a high degree of regard and esteem. But when, as Christians, we believe in a Divine influence and direction, we find abundant cause to conclude, that this influence was extended

* John i. 45.

B 4

to those who wrote or compiled the Scriptures, and therefore believe with the apostle Paul, that they were "given by inspiration of God;"* and are productive of those important advantages which he attaches to them.

But notwithstanding the strong belief, which is generally entertained of the truth of these writings, and of their having been communicated under the influence of Divine inspiration; there are persons, who do not acknowledge one or both of these claims, to that credibility and reverence which are attached to the Scriptures. It will therefore be necessary to pay some attention to the objections advanced by these persons; in doing which, it may be proper, first to consider those which are made against the authenticity of the Scriptures.

These objections may be divided into two classes.

1. To the writings, as the genuine productions of the authors to whom they are ascribed.

2. To the works themselves, as being a true history.

* 2 Tim. iii. 16.

With respect to the objection against their being genuine, in relation to their imputed authors, if it could in some cases be well supported, it would by no means invalidate either the truth or the inspiration of these writings; because the books do not always declare their authors. They have, however, been transmitted through so regular a channel of evidence, by a people for whom they were especially written, and by whom they were religiously preserved, as to render their being written by those to whom they are ascribed, as indubitable as any thing of the kind can be. In some cases the authors may be considered as dubious; and seeing that, in these instances, the books are not imputed in Scripture to any individual, no objection can reasonably be made on this ground.

An objection is sometimes made to the supposed author, on account of his speaking of himself in the third person; but this cannot have much weight, when it is considered that it is a mode of writing not peculiar to the Scriptures, but has been adopted by various historians, whose works have been generally admitted without disputation.

Another more plausible reason for disputing the authors, arises from some places being mentioned by names, which appear to have been given to them subsequent to the alleged writer's existence; or from saying, that a place is called by a particular name "to this day," with other similar expressions. Now all this is easily obviated by considering, what is generally admitted, that, after the Babylonian captivity, Ezra revised the Jewish scriptures; and it appears, that, in some instances, he either made use of modern names, or added remarks of his own to elucidate the history. 'He was a religious character, and one whom the Jews considered as acting under Divine direction, they therefore received his comments, and added them, if he did not do it himself, to the original text. This is a fact which the Jews acknowledge, and which accounts for the causes of this objection in such a manner, as must, I apprehend, be satisfactory to every impartial mind.

The account of the death of Moses, at the end of Deuteronomy, was probably added by Joshua or Samuel, to complete the history of Moses, in those books that were written by him; and is a circumstance, which no reasonable man, who is acquainted with literary publications, would make a ground of objection to the authenticity of any book.

Nor are the objections to the truth of the matters related in the Holy Scriptures, of more weight than those alleged against their authenticity. They arise from some apparent inconsistencies of one part with another, and from a supposed difference in some instances, from other histories.

In most cases, the inconsistencies objected are only in appearance; they may be, and indeed have been, removed by a critical examination of the subjects; and if we admit a few to arise from incorrectness in transcribers or translators, surely no wise man would consider such a circumstance as a reasonable ground, for rejecting even writings much less authenticated than these. As to the few variations from other writers, if they cannot otherwise be reconciled, a fair consideration of the probability, which of them had the best means of information, will, I believe, give a clear preference to the sacred historian. But the Scriptures are, in general, found to be well supported by other

authors; and it is worthy of observation, that
the completion of prophecies recorded in various
parts of holy writ, is confirmed by profane
historians of good credit, who, it must be admitted, could have no inducement to give any
unfair testimony in their favour.*

That some verbal difficulties should occur in
a collection of books, which were written from
more than one thousand seven hundred, to up-
wards of three thousand years ago, and which
contain a history of above four thousand years,
is what may reasonably be expected; but that
writings of such antiquity, should come down to
us so perfect as they appear to be, is cause of
admiration; and, considering their interesting
importance, of gratitude and praise.

Having, I hope, sufficiently obviated the most
plausible objections, that are made against the
truth and credibility of the Scriptures, the next
circumstance to be considered is their Inspiration; by which I understand, that the writers or
compilers were influenced by the Holy Spirit

* For the truth of these assertions, see Grotius on the Truth of
the Christian Religion, 3 Sect. 14 and 16.   Newton on the Prophecies, and Prettyman on the Study of the Bible.

in communicating these writings. A considerable part of them, are given as express communications from the Almighty, to his servants and prophets: this, if we admit the truth of the relation, determines a large proportion of the Bible to be an immediate revelation, which is more, as to the degree, than is necessarily implied by the term inspiration.

The reasons for considering these writings, as being given under that Divine influence which is called inspiration, are the following:

1.—The characters of the writers, all of whom, that we can ascertain, were men, eminently endowed with divine gifts; and who appear to have drawn up these writings for the use and edification of the church of God; in doing which we may reasonably conclude, that his assistance would be sought for and afforded.

2.—The character of Ezra, who, besides being the writer of at least one book, collected the various writings of the Old Testament, with the exception of two or three books not then written.*   His character, gifts, and motives, all

* These are Nehemiah and Malachi, and perhaps Esther, with part of Chronicles. They are generally supposed to have been added by Simon the Just.

lead us to the same conclusion as before; with this addition, that as the occasion, or the authors of some part of these writings, are not clearly ascertained, Ezra's compilation under Divine influence, gives an additional sanction to these books.

3.—The testimony of the apostle Paul, who says, " All scripture is given by inspiration of God, and* is profitable for doctrine," &c.

* I am aware, that some persons endeavour to set aside the force of this passage, by stating that one Greek manuscript omits the και, in English *and*, and that some ancient Versions have no word equivalent to it ; by which they would give a different meaning to the passage. In answer to this, it may be observed,

1.—That for one Greek manuscript which wants the και, or *and*, there are great numbers which have it; and that one is neither so ancient, nor of so good credit as most of the others, in the opinion of many critics. Now, to set all other manuscripts aside, and prefer a single and less authenticated reading, with two or three translations, which, though they may be ancient, can by no means be considered of equal validity with so many copies in the original tongue, would be an exercise of criticism, which nothing but a partial predilection to a preconceived opinion would adopt. Would these critics admit such arguments in favour of the authenticity of 1 John v. 7 ?

2.—The context requires a sense, which implies that the apostle considered that all which he had just called the Holy Scriptures were inspired. Ancient commentators, even those

When we consider the opportunities and abilities of the apostle, for judging in such a case, (to say nothing of his own inspiration,) his testi-

who have made use of the versions which have not the *and*, still consider the passage as implying, that the whole Scripture was Divinely inspired. So that supposing (what however is not admitted) that the *και* was not in the original, the sense is still the same. For the more clear elucidation of the subject, let us read the whole passage, as these objectors would render it. " From a Child thou hast known the Holy Scriptures, which are able to make thee wise unto salvation, through faith which is in Christ Jesus. All scripture (or every writing) given by Inspiration of God, is profitable for doctrine, for reproof, for correction, for instruction in righteousness; that the man of God may be perfect, thoroughly furnished unto all good works."

Now, every one that reads this passage impartially, and considers the construction of the sentences correctly, must, I apprehend, admit, that the Holy Scriptures, mentioned in the beginning of the paragraph, are included in the general observations respecting, " All scripture given by inspiration," or that, " All scripture given by inspiration," only alluded *to* " The holy scriptures" mentioned just before. In either case the inference is clear, that the Scriptures of the Old Testament, which are all that were then called the Holy Scriptures, were considered by the apostle as Divinely inspired; and as answering to the character he gives in the 16th verse. It may be further observed, that without the *και*, the passage may be translated thus : " All (or the whole) scripture being Divinely inspired, is profitable," &c. Even the Latin Vulgate, which is one of the Versions brought forward as favouring the omission of the *and*, will bear this rendering : " Omnis scriptura, divinitus inspirata, utilis est," &c.

mony appears to be an insurmountable argument in favour of those writings, concerning which he made this declaration.

3.—The sense is, however, more clear and unequivocal, by the well supported reading of the word καὶ, or *and*, as given in our translation. This sense contains the reason why the holy scriptures were able to make Timothy wise unto salvation; but supposing the meaning simply to be, that all scripture which is divinely inspired, is profitable, &c. without any connection with the preceding verse, the position would become an unconnected truism ; as no doubt could be entertained, that all scripture which was divinely inspired, was thus profitable. Besides, this meaning would leave Timothy, and every other reader, in uncertainty, which part of the scripture was, and which was not inspired : it offers no rule to distinguish them. But had this been the apostle's meaning, there was a fair occasion, and indeed a call upon him, to offer some means of distinction.

From all these considerations, I am induced to believe, that the construction given by our translators, is supportable, not only by nearly all the Greek manuscripts, but by the just rules of criticism ; and by every other reasonable consideration of which the subject is capable. See this matter farther discussed by Findlay, on the Inspiration of the Jewish Scriptures, in answer to Dr. Geddes.

For the sake of some of my readers, it may be proper to take notice of an objection, which has been made from Robert Barclay having, in his apology, quoted the passage without the *and* : " All scripture given by inspiration of God is profita-

4.—Although the latter arguments are applicable only to the Old Testament; yet the first relates to both; and it is presumed, that none but Jews, who acknowledge the inspiration of the Old Testament, will deny it to the New. The exception which the apostle Paul makes in an instance or two, to his writing by commandment, is a proof of *his* writings at least being Divinely inspired.

After giving these reasons, I shall proceed to consider the principal objections to this inspiration, which I apprehend to be,

ble," &c. In answer to this, it may be observed, that Robert Barclay originally wrote and published his apology in Latin, and I believe generally quoted the texts of Scripture from the Latin Vulgate, of which this is a translation. Even supposing him to have preferred this rendering, yet, if we may judge from what he has written on the Scriptures, there is no reason to believe, he doubted the inspiration of any part of them. He begins his Thesis on the Scriptures thus : " From these revelations of the Spirit of God to the saints, have proceeded the Scriptures of truth ;" and this he applies to the historical, as well as the prophetical, doctrinal, and exhortatory parts of the Old and New Testaments.

It is hoped that the importance of the subject of this note, will excuse its length. To have incorporated it in the body of the work, would not have been so suitable for many readers.

1.—That some of the matters related, are of too trivial a nature, to be the subjects of Divine inspiration.

2.—That some others appear so inconsistent with the nature of the Divine Being, as to render it altogether improbable, that he ever warranted what is there expressed.

With respect to the first objection, I believe we are by no means competent judges. The Old Testament, to which this objection may be principally made, was not primarily written for us of the present day; but for a people, who had many peculiar customs and ceremonies, and to whom many things might be important, that to us may appear of a trifling nature. Nor is it improbable, that much of what these objectors consider as trifling, may to others of their contemporaries, be both important and instructive. The pious and humble mind will often derive instruction from many of the works of Divine Providence, which may be overlooked by the vain and fastidious, as not worthy of their notice.

The second objection, it is apprehended, is meant principally to apply to those passages in the Old Testament, where the Almighty is represented as authorizing the destruction of man by man. This is an objection not only to the inspiration, but to the truth of the Scriptures; and though it appears to be the strong hold of the enemies of the Bible, it is by no means impregnable. It has, indeed, been often attacked and reduced ; but such is their fondness for it, that they are continually rebuilding it, and resorting to it.

In replying to this objection, it may be proper, first, to consider the command of God to Abraham, to offer up his son Isaac, which has been much insisted on, as favouring human sacrifices, and as an argument against the Scriptures. It stands recorded as a trial of Abraham's faith; and as, after his full resignation, his hand was stayed from the performance of the act; I am at a loss to conceive what inference can be drawn from this circumstance, derogatory to the character of the Divine Being, or of those writings which represent Him, as putting the righteous patriarch's love and obedience to this great trial. Had the sacrifice been actually made, the objection to it might have had more appearance of validity; but as the case is represented, and no doubt rightly represented, it appears to afford an argument against, rather than for, human sacrifices. The conduct of Abraham is mentioned, in both the Old and the New Testaments, with the most marked approbation : and it has obtained for the obedient patriarch the distinguished character of, " the friend of God."*

The command given to the Israelites, to make war on the Canaanites, and to destroy them, is an objection, which, it is difficult to conceive, can be seriously urged by those who consider war to be lawful, even under the Christian dispensation. War is generally allowed to be one of those judgments, by which Divine Providence hath often afflicted a guilty nation; and, in the instances on which the objection is founded, this appears to have been remarkably the case. They were indeed judgments which had been mercifully protracted. Thus we read, that the possession of the promised land by Abraham, or his posterity, was deferred for several generations, because " the iniquity of the Amorites was not yet full;"† although there is reason to believe from this expression, as well as from other circumstances, that their sins were then very great.

* James ii. 23.   † Gen. xv. 16.

ON THE HOLY SCRIPTURES. 33

This is farther elucidated by the command given to the Israelties, to abstain from many evil practices, (some of them of the grossest kind) of which the nations whom they were to expel, were guilty. These Moses plainly mentions as the cause of their expulsion ; warning the Israelites at the same time against similar conduct, which would produce similar judgments : " Defile not ye yourselves in any of these things ; for in all these things the nations are defiled, which I cast out before you. And the land is defiled ; therefore I do visit the iniquity thereof upon it; and the land itself vomiteth out her inhabitants. Ye shall therefore keep my statutes and my judgments, and shall not commit any of these abominations; that the land spue not you out also, when ye defile it, as it spued out the nations that were before you."*

This subject is also placed in a clear and forcible point of view by the remonstrance of Moses, as related in the ninth chapter of Deuteronomy; where, after cautioning the people against any presumptuous conceits of their own merits, he expressly says to them : " Not for thy righteousness, or for the uprightness of thy

* Lev. xviii. 24.

heart, dost thou go to possess the land ; but for the wickedness of these nations, doth the Lord thy God drive them out before thee."*

The case of Agag has also been brought forward to support the objection, which we have now under consideration ; but in this instance, we have again a cause assigned for the judgment executed : "As thy sword hath made women childless, so shall thy mother be childless among women."† From this expression there is reason to suppose, that Agag had been remarkable for his violence and cruelty, which brought this judgment justly upon him.

It has been alleged, that these pretensions to Divine commands were only a cloak for ambition and cruelty But this cannot reasonably be supposed to be the case, when it is considered that these judgments were not confined to the heathen nations ; but that similiar ones were also threatened and executed upon the Israelites themselves. Although they were a people distinguished by many peculiar favours ; yet, when they departed from the law and commandment of their God, and degenerated into idolatry and

* Deut. ix. 5. † 1 Sam. xv. 33.

wickedness, they became the subjects of Divine retribution. Thus the prophet Isaiah expostulates with them : " Who gave Jacob for a spoil, and Israel to the robbers ? Did not the Lord, he against whom we have sinned ? For they would not walk in his ways, neither were they obedient unto his law ; therefore he hath poured upon him the fury of his anger, and the strength of battle."* Even Moses, their leader in these supposed schemes of ambition, denounced, in the most ample manner, the judgments, which would be the consequence of their disobedience to the law of their God.—See Lev. xxvi. 14, &c. Deut. xxviii. 15, &c.

When we consider the peculiar humility and disinterestedness of Moses, in refusing to be called the son of Pharoah's daughter ; in the great reluctance with which he accepted the government of the Israelites ; in prefering their forgiveness and preservation to his own aggrandizement, or that of his family ; and in the singular liberality which he manifested, when Eldad and Medad were complained of, for prophesying in the camp ; when these circumstances are considered, there seems no ground whatever to

* Isaiah xlii. 24.

suspect Moses of either ambition or cruelty. We perceive, on the contrary, the propriety of the distinguished character given of him, most probably by some pious transcriber of the Pentateuch : " Now the man Moses was very meek, above all the men which lived on the face of the earth."*

In considering the various circumstances connected with this subject, there appears to be abundant cause to acknowledge that the Lord's ways are equal, and that those judgments upon the Canaanites, were not the exercise of a capricious severity; but were administered under circumstances, which perfectly reconcile them to those principles of justice and mercy, which we consider among the most distinguished attributes of the Deity. And though, in many instances, the innocent may seem to suffer equally with the guilty ; yet this is no more than is generally the case in other public calamities. Even in those most remarkable ones, the universal deluge, and the destruction of Sodom and Gomorrah, many innocent children must have suffered with their guilty parents. In considering these cases, we should remember,

* Numbers xii. 3.

ON THE HOLY SCRIPTURES.   37

that whatever public afflictions may be directed
for the punishment of nations, it is to a future life
that we must look for the grand distinction between individuals; when " God will render to
every man according to his deeds."*

If some of those, who, with myself, consider
war altogether inconsistent with the Christian
dispensation, should argue from the unchange-
ableness of the Divine nature, that the Almighty
could not allow of, or enjoin practices, in one
age, which are inconsistent in another; it may
and ought to be observed, that, in his dispensations to mankind, great variety is evident; and
many things which were not only allowed, but
commanded, in former times, and under different
circumstances, would now be improper.

It also appears, that when our blessed Lord
set forth the peaceableness of the gospel dispensation, he showed that a contrary conduct had
been more than permitted in former times; and
unless we intend to controvert the propriety of
the manner, in which the Author of the Christian religion propagated it, we must allow, that
there have been times, in which divers things

* Rom. ii. 6.

were lawful that are now unlawful; and thus we
may reconcile the consistency of the Jewish wars
with the Divine will. "Ye have heard that it
hath been said, an eye for an eye, and a tooth
for a tooth; but I say unto you, resist not evil."
Again, "Ye have heard that it hath been said,
Thou shalt love thy neighbour, and hate thine
enemy;* but I say unto you, Love your enemies,"
&c. Now, when we consider the expressions
just cited, and observe the obvious difference
they make between the dispensations of the law
and of the Gospel; we may find abundant reason
to believe, that it was not inconsistent with the
Divine nature and will, to command those things
which are related respecting the wars of the
Jews.

If any credibility is due to the writings of
Moses, and they have all the claim to credibility
which writings of that antiquity well can have;
it is evident that those wars were commanded
by the Almighty. And when we consider, that
we have no less support for the authority of
Moses than our Lord himself; that he and his

* The words " hate thine enemy," do not appear in the Old
Testament; perhaps they were added by the scribes as a gloss;
however, our Lord, by his recital, acknowledges them as not inconsistent with the former dispensation.

apostles mention him with evident tokens of their considering him Divinely directed; we, must, in denying the authority of Moses, also deny that of Christ and his apostles. A consequence, from the idea of which every Christian must revolt.

Let us, therefore, be content with that evidence of the Divine will which is afforded us; and, rather than impugn the former dispensations of God to mankind, be thankful to Him for having introduced one so much more excellent, in which—"Glory to God in the highest," is peculiarly united with—"Peace on earth, and good will to men."

But whilst I have been endeavouring to remove these objections, I have regretted that there should be any necessity, thus to "justify the ways of God to men," as recorded in holy writ, and to endeavour to support the cause of that Omnipotent Being, whose prerogative alone it is—"That he giveth no account of any of his matters." He has, notwithstanding, as far as different circumstances will permit, condescended to adapt his dispensations towards mankind, to those principles of wisdom, justice, and mercy, which are the rules of our conduct towards each other. If, in some instances, we cannot perceive this consistency, the infinite disparity between the Divine Being and his creature man, might reasonably induce us to expect difficulties of this kind ; and surely the wisdom, no more than the faith, of those is to be admired, who reject every thing respecting an Infinite Being, that does not comport with their finite capacities. " Canst thou, by search-ing, find out God ? Canst thou find out the Almighty to perfection ? It is as high as heaven; what canst thou do ? Deeper than hell ; what canst thou know ? The measure thereof is longer than the earth, and broader than the sea. If he cut off, and shut up, and gather together, then who can hinder him?"*

But in admitting the Holy Scriptures, to have been communicated to us under Divine in-fluence or inspiration, it is not necessary to consider all that is related in them, concerning even those whose general conduct might entitle them to the character of good men, as intended for our imitation. In many instances, indeed, their conduct is very properly and impartially

* Job xi. 7.

censured; and this impartiality constitutes one
of the many excellencies of the bible. But
there are also circumstances simply related,
without any comment, which it is by no means
requisite to consider as related with approbation, or authorising a similar conduct in us. A
close and critical examination of some of these
cases, would probably remove much of the
impression which a slighter consideration may
have sometimes produced. At any rate, neither
the sacred historian, nor that inspiration under
which he is supposed to write, is chargeable
with such circumstances.—Here, however, we
have again occasion for the exercise of our
gratitude, in that it has pleased Divine Providence to give us an existence under a dispensation, which requires singular degrees of purity
and uprightness of conduct; and which exceeds
all former ones in the excellence of its morality,
as well as in the peculiar peaceableness of its
principles, and the spirituality of its worship.

Great judgment is also necessary in applying
the Scriptures to the support of religious doctrines and observances. These have been. I apprehend, sometimes adopted from what may be
incidentally mentioned, rather than inculcated.

In considering the Scriptures, and endeavouring to build systems upon them, it requires great care to distinguish those things which are universal and essential, from such as are only of a temporary or local nature. For want of an attention of this kind, many unprofitable disputes, (to say no worse of them,) have arisen among the professors of Christianity; and much unnecessary stress has been laid on things which the Christian religion does not enjoin or require.

Highly however as those writings are to be valued, and highly indeed we do esteem them! there is not only a possibility, but a danger of placing too much dependance upon them, by preferring them to that Divine Spirit from which they proceed, to which they direct our attention, and by which only they can be rightly opened to our understandings. Thus the Jews, in the days of our blessed Saviour's personal appearance on earth, paid great attention to the Scriptures; and at the same time did not believe in Him, "of whom Moses in the law, and the prophets did write." On this account our Lord reproves them in this manner: "Search (or, ye search) the scriptures; for in them ye think ye have eternal life; and they are they which testify of me; and ye will not come unto me, that ye might have life." Now, that from which the Scriptures proceeded, and to which they amply bear witness as the means of salvation, is what we apprehend there is a danger of neglecting; and thereby of dwelling upon the letter, without a proper regard to the Spirit; a danger against which the Scriptures themselves contain many salutary cautions.

There is also a name by which the Holy Scriptures are frequently distinguished, which appears to be, in divers respects, exceptionable, namely: "The Word of God." This is an appellation which is otherwise applied in those writings; and it tends to create a confusion of ideas, unnecessarily to denominate several subjects by the same name. Christ is called, " The Word of God."* The term † is also applied to that holy principle or Spirit, by which he carries on the work of salvation in the hearts of true Christians; and frequently to the preaching of the gospel; but by applying it to the sacred writings, a misapplication of passages in them is frequently occasioned. That these writings contain the words of God, we readily ad-

* John i. 1, &c.   Rev. xix. 13.
† Heb. iv 12; 1 Pet. i, 23 ; 1 John ii. 14.

mit; but we think it safest, as well as most proper, to designate them by that appellation, by which the apostle Paul has distinguished them; and, by way of priority to all other writings, to style them, The Holy Scriptures. Concerning these writings we believe with this apostle, that they were "given by inspiration of God; and are profitable for doctrine, for reproof, for correction, for instruction in righteousness; that the man of God may be perfect, thoroughly furnished unto all good works."*

* 2 Tim. iii. 16.

CHAP. III.

ON THE CHRISTIAN RELIGION.

The Fall of Man, and the Promise of a Redeemer.—Different modes of Divine communication to Man.—Prospects and Prophecies of the Gospel Day.—Christ comes among the Jews.—The benefits of his coming designed to be universal.—Objects of his coming recapitulated.—Christian redemption a work of love.—Divinity of Christ and of the Holy Spirit.—On the Trinity.—Justification.—Resurrection.—Arguments and Evidences of Christianity.—The true and perfect Christian.

HAVING vindicated the truth and Divine authority of the Scriptures, we next proceed to consider the most important doctrines of the Christian religion.

Man having, by disobedience to the Divine command, lost that state of innocence and purity in which he was originally created ; and having thereby subjected himself and his offspring, to sin and misery ; it pleased his gracious and merciful Creator, in the riches of his love, early to point out and to promise a Redeemer. This was done at the very time when sentence was

c 5

pronounced on our first parents for their transgression; for then their tempter and seducer received this judgment : " I will put enmity between thee and the woman ; and between thy seed and her seed ; it shall bruise thy head, and thou shalt bruise his heel."*

But notwithstanding the promise was thus early made, many ages elapsed before it pleased God completely to fulfil it: during which time, however, he did not leave mankind wholly to themselves ; but, by the ministration of angels ; by that holy Spirit which was more plentifully to be poured forth in the Christian dispensation, and by other means, he communicated his will to the children of men ; striving with and reproving the ungodly because of their iniquities, as well as exhorting and comforting the righteous under those trials, unto which this probationary state, and, in some instances, the love and the fear of their God rendered them liable. Typical offerings and sacrifices for sin were also established, in allusion to that one offering, by which " He hath now perfected for ever them that are sanctified."†

Among other sources of consolation, was the prospect, which was at times given to the patri-

* Gen. iii. 15.   † Heb. x. 14.

archs and prophets, of the day of Christ, and of the excellence of his dispensation; concerning which we have many predictions left upon record, abundantly setting forth those advantages which were designed to mankind by Him, whom we have represented to us as the Sent of the Father. By these prophecies, as well as by the types of the Mosaic law, the minds of many were gradually prepared for the reception of the promised Messiah; and many there appear to have been, who, with Simeon and Anna, " waited for the consolation of Israel, and looked for redemption in Jerusalem,"* by the coming of Him, who was peculiarly prophesied of, as " A light to lighten the Gentiles;" as well as for " The glory of his people Israel."§

Thus, " When the fulness of the time was come, God sent forth his Son, made of a woman, made under the law, to redeem them that were under the law,"† from those ceremonious observances, which were designed to be as a " Schoolmaster to bring them to Christ."‡ Yet the great object of Christ's coming was by no means confined to the Jewish people; amongst

* Luke ii. 25, 38.
§ Isaiah xlii. 6.   Luke ii. 32.   † Gal. iv. 4.
‡ Gal. iii. 24.

whom, and by whom, he suffered that igno-
minious death, by which it hath pleased God,
(and surely it ought to suffice us, that it has
thus pleased him,) " To reconcile all things to
himself."*

The evangelical prophet, above seven hundred years before our Saviour's personal appearance on earth, speaking in the name of the
Almighty, declares : " It is a light thing, that
thou shouldst be my servant, to raise up the
tribes of Jacob, and to restore the preserved of
Israel : I will also give thee for a light to the
Gentiles, that thou mayest be my salvation unto
the end of the earth."† Consonant with this
gracious prediction, are these declarations of
the apostle John : " In him was life ; and the
life was the light of men." " That was the
true light, which lighteth every man that cometh
into the world."‡ " He is the propitiation for
our sins ; and not for ours only, but also for the
sins of the whole world."§ Many are the prophecies concerning the universal extent of the
benefits of Christ's coming, the accomplishment
of which is fully borne witness to by the writers
of the New Testament. This is particularly

_____

* Col. i. 20.   † Isaiah xlix. 6.   ‡ John i. 4, 9.
§ 1 John ii. 2.

and frequently done by Paul, who, being in an especial manner the apostle of the Gentiles, has abundantly set forth : "That the Gentiles should be fellow-heirs, and of the same body, and partakers of his promise in Christ Jesus by the Gospel."* Thus was broken down that partition wall, which formerly existed between Jews and Gentiles ; all were united in one common cause ; and all had an equal interest in Him, with whom "There is neither Greek nor Jew ; circumcision nor uncircumcision ; Barbarian, Scythian, bond nor free ; male nor female ; but Christ is all, and in all ; and all are one in Christ."†

From what has already been expressed, it appears evident, that the love of God, in sending his Son into the world, was not limited to any part of it ; but that the benefits were designed to extend, as far as the effects of Adam's transgression. This the apostle shows in the 5th chapter of the epistle to the Romans ; and in another epistle, speaking of the resurrection of the dead, he asserts : that, "As in Adam all die, even so in Christ shall all be made alive."‡ It affords one of the most encouraging consi-

* Ephes. iii. 6.   † Col. iii. 11.   Gal. iii. 28.
‡ 1 Cor. xv. 22.

derations, that these benefits are thus unlimited, and that through the propitiatory sacrifice of our blessed Redeemer; and by that Spirit, the more plentiful effusion of which he hath purchased for mankind; the advantages resulting from his death may be received, even by those, whose situation may deprive them of the opportunity of an external knowledge of the truths of the gospel.

Unless we admit this, we shall greatly contract the benefits of Christ's coming. He "Tasted death for every man."* His "Light lighteth every man that cometh into the world."† And, although the outward knowledge of these gospel truths may be withheld from many, yet their operation is not therefore necessarily frustrated. How many partake of favours of which they cannot trace the cause! He, who is not willing that any should perish, has doubtless provided means by which the state of perdition may be avoided, even by those to whom his Providence, has not afforded opportunities to obtain a historical knowledge of the truths of Christianity. Those, however, who are in possession of this knowledge, cannot be too thankful for it; in that they are enabled to draw nigh

* Heb. ii. 9. † John i. 9.

unto God with more full assurance of faith; and, confiding in their blessed Redeemer, are encouraged, under their various conflicts and exercises, to look unto Him who is " Touched with the feeling of our infirmities,"* and " Is able to succour those that are tempted."†

The Christian religion then teaches, that our first parents having sinned and lost the Divine image, the fallen nature became so predominant, that it was by them transferred to their offspring: but in order that man might be restored to favour, and to a state of purity, it pleased the Almighty to promise and send a Redeemer, whose sacrifice of himself he saw meet to accept, as the means of reconciliation and forgiveness of sins; hereby putting an end to all those sacrifices, which, from the fall, or very soon after, to the time when Christ thus offered up himself, had been adopted as the means of obtaining acceptance with God. And although we cannot trace this practice to a Divine command, earlier than the time of Moses; yet the universal adoption of it by the religious of all ages, is a strong implication that it was of Divine origin, instituted in reference to that " One of-

* Heb. iv. 15.　　　† Heb. ii. 18.

fering, by which God hath perfected for ever them that are sanctified."*

Thus, the chief objects of the coming of Christ, evidently appear to have been, first, by the sacrifice of himself, to make atonement to God for us, and to become the Mediator between God and man. Secondly, by the sanctifying operation of the Holy Spirit—"To finish transgression, and to make an end of sins, and to bring in everlasting righteousness."† And thirdly, by putting an end to the legal dispensation, and as the apostle expresses it, "Blotting out the hand-writing of ordinances that was against us,"‡ to lead mankind to a more pure and spiritual worship of the Divine Being.

It also appears that the Christian redemption is throughout a work of love. "God so *loved* the world, that he gave his only begotten Son, that whosoever believeth in him should not perish but have everlasting life."§ In this point of view, we contemplate this interesting and important subject; and not as the effect of implacable wrath, as some represent it. Christ was and is the gift of God. Thus the Holy

* Heb. x. 14.   † Dan. ix. 24.   ‡ Col. ii. 14.
§ John iii. 16.

Scriptures represent the subject to us ; and surely, the greater the gift, the greater the love. " God commendeth his love towards us, in that while we were yet sinners, Christ died for us."* He co-operated with the Father in this gracious design ; and though he was of the same Divine nature, he condescended to take upon Him our human nature, and " was made flesh and dwelt among us,"† until he had by his life, and by his death, as man, completed the work that was given him to do ; after which he ascended to that glory, which he had with the Father before the world began.

Here we are led to consider the Divinity of our blessed Saviour, in which we, as a people, do most surely believe ; but as every thing relating to the Divine Being, which is not expressly revealed, is far above the reach of human comprehension, we are desirous of avoiding all such particular disquisitions, as lead beyond the clear expression of holy writ. We can indeed say on this, as on every other occasion, that we believe all that the Scriptures have spoken and inculcated we believe that the evangelist was clearly speaking of Jesus Christ, and of his Divinity or Godhead, when he said : " In the

* Rom. v. 8.　　　† John i. 14.

beginning was the Word, and the Word was
with God, and the Word was God. The
same was in the beginning with God. All
things were made by Him, and without Him
was not any thing made that was made. In
Him was life, and the life was the light of
men."* "And the Word was made flesh and
dwelt among us."† Here we have a clear and
full testimony both to the Divinity and the humanity of Christ; and we have, ever since we
were a people, borne testimony to this Scripture
doctrine.

We likewise believe in the Divinity of the
Holy Spirit, which is frequently united in Scripture with the Father and with the Son ; and
whose office, in the instruction and salvation of
mankind, is set forth in divers passages of holy
writ. See Matt. xxviii. 19. John xv. 26.
Acts xxviii. 25. Heb. ix. 14.

This belief in the Divinity of the Father, the
Son, and the Holy Spirit, induced some of the
teachers in the Christian church, about three
hundred years after the personal appearance of
Christ, to form a doctrine to which they gave
the name of Trinity ; but in our writings we

* John i. 1 to 4.   † Ibid 14.

seldom make use of this term, thinking it best, on such a subject, to keep to scriptural expressions, and to avoid those disputes which have since perplexed the Christian world, and led into speculations beyond the power of human abilities to decide. If we consider that we ourselves are composed of a union of " spirit, and soul and body,"* and yet cannot determine how even these are united ; how much less may we expect perfect clearness on a subject, so far above our finite comprehension, as that of the Divine Nature.

After expressing our sentiments on what is called the Trinity, it will be proper to explain our views of the doctrine of justification, concerning which so much diversity of sentiment prevails ; some imputing it wholly to faith, and others principally if not wholly to works.

So far as remission of sins, and a capacity to receive salvation, are parts of justification, we attribute it to the sacrifice of Christ ; " in whom we have redemption through his blood, the forgiveness of sins, according to the riches of his grace."† But when we consider justification as a state of Divine favour and acceptance, we

* 1 Thess, v. 23.   † Eph. l. 7.

ascribe it, not simply either to faith or works, but to the sanctifying operation of the Spirit of Christ, from which only living faith and acceptable works proceed; and by which we may come to know, that "the Spirit itself beareth witness with our spirits, that we are the children of God."*

In attributing our justification, through the grace of God in Christ Jesus, to the operation of the Holy Spirit, which sanctifies the heart, and produces the work of regeneration, we are supported by the testimony of the Apostle Paul, who says: "Not by works of righteousness which we have done, but of his mercy he saved us, by the washing of regeneration, and renewing of the Holy Ghost."† Again, "But ye are washed, but ye are sanctified, but ye are justified, in the name of the Lord Jesus, and by the Spirit of our God."‡

By this view of the doctrine of justification, we conceive the apparently different sentiments of the apostles Paul and James are reconciled. Neither of them say, that faith alone, or works alone, are the cause of our being justified; but as one of them asserts the necessity of faith,

---

* Rom. viii. 16.   † Titus iii. 5..   ‡ 1 Cor. vi. 11.

and the other of works, for effecting this great object, a clear and convincing proof is afforded that both contribute to our justification; and that faith without works, and works without faith, are equally dead.

The doctrine of the resurrection of the dead, is so connected with the Christian religion, that it will be also proper to say something on this subject. In explaining our belief of this doctrine, we refer to the xvth chapter of the 1st Epistle to the Corinthians. In this chapter is clearly laid down the resurrection of a body, though not of the same body that dies. " There are celestial bodies, and there are bodies terrestrial; but the glory of the celestial is one, and the glory of the terrestrial is another. So also is the resurrection of the dead.—It is sown a natural body, it is raised a spiritual body: there is a natural body and there is a spiritual body. Now this I say, brethren, that flesh and blood cannot inherit the kingdom of God, neither doth corruption inherit incorruption."* Here we rest our belief in this " mystery," without desiring to pry into it beyond what is revealed to us; remembering that " secret things belong

* 1 Cor. xv. 40, 42, 44, 50.

unto the Lord our God; but those things which are revealed, belong unto us, and to our children."*

Many are the aguments and evidences which might be brought forward in favour of the Christian religion; but none appears to be more forcible, than the purity of that morality which is inculcated by it; and which is most effectually adapted to the promotion of the happiness of mankind in this world, as well as in that which is to come. A just test of principles, as well as of men, was laid down by our Saviour in these words: "By their fruits ye shall know them."† It is the conduct to which principles lead, by which we are to judge of their rectitude; rather than by the actions of men, who may profess these principles, but whose weakness may often cause a violation of them. Now, to apply this test to Christ and his religion, let us first attend to that angelic song, with which his birth was introduced into the world: "Glory to God in the highest, and on earth peace; good will towards men."‡ Next, let us consider how his precepts and his example corresponded with it. Read that most excellent sermon on

* Deut. xxix. 29.   † Matt. vii. 20.   ‡ Luke ii. 14.

ON THE CHRISTIAN RELIGION. 59

the mount ; look at the example he has left us, under all the temptations and trials which, for our sakes, were permitted to assail him. With what firmness did he reprove the vices and hypocrisy of the Jews! With what meekness did he bear their insults and persecutions! Truly, indeed, was it foretold of him : " He is brought as a lamb to the slaughter; and as a sheep before her shearers is dumb, so he openeth not his mouth."* And when this people had executed upon him all that their malice could devise, He, consistently with the precepts which he had inculcated, in return for all their injuries, put up this most affecting prayer; "Father! forgive them ; they know not what they do."†

But this example and these precepts were not confined to our holy head and high priest. In that part of conduct which is the most difficult for human nature, the forgiveness of injuries, we find the proto-martyr, Stephen, followed his Lord's example ; and, when expiring under the cruelties of the same people, thus poured out his soul unto God: "Lord! lay not this sin to their charge."‡ What other religion

* Isaiah liii. 7.—This whole chapter is a remarkable prediction of the coming and sufferings of Christ.

† Luke xxiii. 34. ‡ Acts vii. 60.

is there, that inculcates a conduct like this! that teaches not only to forgive injuries, but even to pray for those that are the cause of them! Precepts which alone give a decided preference to Christianity, above all other religions in the world!

Let us next look into those epistles, which the apostles addressed to the Christian converts, both among the Jews and Gentiles; and there we shall again find, in addition to the doctrinal part of Christianity, such a spirit of pure morality and true love, so uniformly inculcated, and the duties of every station in life taught with so much simplicity and energy, as to render the reading of them pleasing and instructive; and at the same time gaining the assent of our judgment, however remote from them our practice may frequently be. The following extract from the Epistle to the Romans is brought forward, not because it contains matter superior to many other parts of the epistles; but because of the conciseness, the simplicity, and the energy, with which the important precepts are conveyed: "Let love be without dissimulation. Abhor that which is evil; cleave to that which is good. Be kindly affectioned one to another with brotherly love; in honour preferring one another; not slothful in business; fervent in spirit; serving the Lord; rejoicing in hope; patient in tribulation; continuing instant in prayer; distributing to the necessity of the saints; given to hospitality. Bless them which persecute you: bless and curse not. Rejoice with them that do rejoice; and weep with them that weep. Be of the same mind one towards another. Mind not high things, but conde- scend to men of low estate. Be not wise in your own conceits. Recompence to no man evil for evil. Provide things honest in the sight of all men. If it be possible, as much as lieth in you, live peaceably with all men."*—"Be not overcome of evil, but overcome evil with good."†

It may not be necessary to enter much into those arguments, which the miracles performed by Christ and his apostles, afford for the truth of the Christian religion. If what is advanced in favour of the truth and credibility of the Holy Scriptures, be admitted, these arguments must unavoidably strike every considerate and impar- tial mind, with irresistible force. It may, how- ever, be proper to observe, that the credibility of these accounts, so far at least as they relate

* Rom. xii. 9 to 18. † Ib. xii. 21. D

to our blessed Saviour, receives great additional force, by being confirmed, in many parts, by four different testimonies, whose distinct concurring evidence, affords no small confirmation of the truth of their relations. This confirmation is rather increased than lessened, by the slight variations which sometimes appear ; for, by these variations, no suspicion can reasonably be fixed of a preconcerted design to impose upon the world. Two of the evangelists, at least, were witnesses of what they wrote ; a third tells us, that he was one of those who received information from such, as from the beginning, were eye witnesses and ministers of the word ; and the fourth is supposed to have written when in company with the apostle Peter, and to have received his information and instruction from him. To these relations of the evangelists the following declaration and testimony of Peter afford additional confirmation : " We have not followed cunningly devised fables, when we made known to you the power and coming of our Lord Jesus Christ; but were eye-witnesses of his Majesty; for he received from God the Father honour and glory, when there came such a voice from the excellent glory : This is my beloved Son, in whom I am well pleased."*

* 2 Peter 1. 16, 17.

In whatever point of view, therefore, we consider the Christian religion, it exhibits to us a
plan and design worthy of our great and gracious Creator; and so well adapted to the state
of the human heart, that nothing appears to be
wanting, but the acceptance of the terms on
which it is offered. Yet as the condition on which
only we can be true Christians, requires us to
deny ourselves, and take up a daily cross to our
evil propensities, this doctrine and that foundation on which it is built, are now, as formerly,
to some a stumbling block, and to others, foolishness. It is indeed to be feared, that many
who adopt the Christian religion in theory, are
but little acquainted with it in practice. True
Christianity is more adapted to the heart, than
to the head : it is not so much a system of doctrines, as it is the power of God unto salvation.
Nevertheless, it necessarily includes doctrines;
but then it requires a union of the spirit with
the letter; of faith and of works; of the power
and of the form of godliness. To unite these
in our hearts, and in our actions, is what appears to me to constitute the true and perfect
Christian.

CHAPTER IV.

ON THE INFLUENCES OF THE HOLY SPIRIT.

The Gift of the Spirit an essential of Christianity.—Different names for the Spirit.—Necessity of its assistance—universally afforded—and in all ages—but most plentifully in the Gospel—Unconditional election and reprobation disowned and disproved.

IN the preceding chapter, the gift of the Holy Spirit has been considered as an essential part of true Christianity; but as it is a doctrine on which we insist,* more than other professors

---

* The word "insist," is here used, because it is not a doctrine peculiar to us, but only one on which we lay more stress than most other Christians. The church of England holds the doctrine much as we do, as may be seen in the liturgy, from which are extracted the two following collects, and to which others of a similar tendency might be added, "The fifth Sunday after Easter." — "O Lord! from whom all good things do come, grant to us, thy humble servants that *by thy holy inspiration*, we may think those things that be good; and *by thy merciful guiding* may perform the same, through our Lord Jesus Christ, *Amen.*" "The 19th Sunday after Trinity." — "O God! forasmuch as without thee we are unable to please thee; mercifully grant that *thy Holy Spirit may in all things direct and rule* our hearts, through," &c.—See also Knox's Christian Philosophy.

of the Christian name, I have apprehended it proper to appropriate a chapter to this subject; and, for that reason, have said less upon it, than I should otherwise have done, when treating of the general doctrines of Christianity.

There are different names in the Scriptures, by which this Spirit is denominated. It is not only called the Holy Spirit, or the Spirit of God, and of Christ; but it is also distinguished, with great propriety, by the appellation of, "the Grace of God;"* as being a mark of His peculiar favour to mankind. Another appropriate denomination is "Light," by which are evinced its effects, in manifesting what is good and what is evil: "For whatsoever doth make manifest is Light."† Other names might be enumerated by which the same thing is distinguished; but these may be sufficient to convey a clear idea of what I have in view.

The Holy Scriptures so frequently make mention of this Divine influence; and enforce it with

* In some instances, the word grace in Scripture simply means favour; but in others, it evidently implies an inward operative principle, and is synonymous with the Holy Spirit.—See Cruden's and Taylor's Concordances, under Grace.

† Ephes. v. 13.

3 D

so much energy that there is no doctrine derived from these writings, on which they appear to be more clear and explicit, and to afford less room for objection and controversy.

In considering this subject, it may be proper to advance and support the following positions.

1.—The necessity of the assistance of the Holy Spirit, for understanding the things, and for working the works, of God.

2.—That such a portion of this Spirit, as is necessary for working out the soul's salvation, is afforded to mankind universally.

With regard to the first position, the apostle Paul argues the case so forcibly, and with such logical clearness, that I shall quote his words, both as the best arguments and the best authority, that can be adduced on the occasion: "What man," saith he "knoweth the things of a man, save the spirit of man which is in him? even so the things of God knoweth no man, but the Spirit of God."* After which he proceeds thus: "Now we have received, not the spirit of the world, but the Spirit which is of God;

* 1 Cor. ii. 11.

that we might know the things that are freely given to us of God : which things also we speak, not in the words which man's wisdom teacheth, but which the Holy Ghost teacheth ; comparing spiritual things with spiritual. But the natural man receiveth not the things of the Spirit of God ; for they are foolishness unto him ; neither can he know them, because they are spiritually discerned."*

In the epistle to the Romans, the apostle also shows the necessity of the assistance of the Spirit, saying expressly : "If any man have not the Spirit of Christ, he is none of his—for as many as are led by the Spirit of God, they are the sons of God : for ye have not received the spirit of bondage again to fear, but ye have received the spirit of adoption, whereby we cry, Abba, Father. The Spirit itself beareth witness with our spirit, that we are the children of God.—Likewise, the Spirit also helpeth our infirmities; for we know not what we should pray for as we ought; but the Spirit itself maketh intercession for us, with groanings which cannot be uttered."†

From these passages, and from many others which might be adduced, it appears clearly,

* 1 Cor. ii. 12—14.   † Rom. viii. 9, 14, 15, 16, 26.

that the influence of the Holy Spirit, is necessary for the performance of those duties, which
make us truly acceptable unto God. It is by
our humble attention to this Spirit, that we are
instructed in these duties, and enabled to perform them; and, by abiding under its purifying
influences, we are gradually created anew in
Christ Jesus, unto good works. By this Spirit
we are also instructed in the great and solemn
duty of prayer : " Praying always with all prayer
and supplication in the Spirit, and watching
thereunto with all perseverance."* It is likewise by this Spirit, that those who are called to
the sacred office of gospel ministry, are "made
able ministers of the New Testament; not of
the letter, but of the Spirit; for the letter
killeth, but the Spirit giveth life."†

In addition to these clear and forcible declarations, it may be proper to remark, that
they are grounded on such arguments, as evince
them not to be confined, to the times of the
apostles, or primitive Christians; but being
adapted to the weakness of man, they may reasonably be supposed to last as long as that
weakness remains : and unless it can be proved
that, since those times, mankind have received

* Ephes. vi. 18.   † 2 Cor. iii. 6.

such an extraordinary accession of natural powers, as makes religion and virtue more easily attained than formerly, we should thankfully submit to be instructed and assisted by the same supernatural means, which the Holy Scriptures so strongly recommend, as essential to the performance of those religious duties, which we owe to our great Creator, and to our merciful Redeemer.

We come now to the second position, viz. that such a portion of the Holy Spirit, as is necessary for working out the soul's salvation, is afforded to mankind universally.

It has already been shown, that there are different names by which this Spirit is distinguished. We apprehend it to be a degree of the same, which the apostle alluded to, when, writing to the Romans respecting the state of the Gentile world, he says: " For when the Gentiles, which have not the law, do by nature the things contained in the law ; these having not the law, are a law unto themselves, which show the work of the law written in their hearts ; their consciences also bearing witness; and their thoughts the meanwhile accusing, or else excusing one another."*

* Rom. ii. 1 and 15.
D 5

We also find that the Spirit of God strove with the antediluvian world, respecting which the Almighty gave this declaration : "My Spirit shall not always strive with man."* Concerning the Jews in the Mosaic dispensation, Nehemiah expresses himself thus in his prayer : "Thou gavest also thy good Spirit to instruct them."† And by Isaiah it is said : "They rebelled and vexed his Holy Spirit; therefore he was turned to be their enemy.‡

Thus we see, in every age and state of the world, there has been a secret principle at work in the minds of men, which formed the basis of all true religion; and by inattention and disobedience to which, they fell into those enormities that produced the just judgments of an offended God. We believe that this Divine principle is, as has already been intimated, the same with that which the Evangelist John calls, " the true light, which lighteth every man that cometh into the world ;"§ that it is the gospel which Paul says, " was preached to [or in ‖] every creature which is under heaven;"¶ and that it is what he elsewhere styles, "the Grace of God, which

---

* Gen. vi. 3.   † Neh. ix. 20.   ‡ Isaiah lxiii. 10.

§ John i. 9.   ‖ The Greek is "ἐντάσῃ τῇ κλίσει"
¶ Col. i. 23.

bringeth salvation, and has appeared unto all men."*

But although this Divine principle has always been in degree, afforded to mankind ; yet it was by the gospel dispensation, that not only life and immortality were brought to light ; but that the Holy Spirit was more plentifully poured forth, and became as it were the leading feature of that religion, which our blessed Redeemer has introduced into the world. With this view of the subject, I apprehend, the Evangelist expresses himself thus : "The Holy Ghost was not yet given, because that Jesus was not yet glorified."† And in another place : "The law was given by Moses ; but Grace and Truth came by Jesus Christ."‡ Of this Grace the apostle Paul, in particular, frequently speaks in his epistles ; but most fully in that to Titus, in the passage just referred to. This passage it may be proper here to give at large : "The Grace of God that bringeth salvation, hath appeared to all men ; teaching us, that denying ungodliness and worldly lusts, we should live soberly, righteously, and godly, in this present world ; looking for that blessed hope, and the glorious appearing of the great God and our Saviour

* Tit. ii. 11. † John vii. 39. ‡ John i. 17.

Jesus Christ; who gave himself for us, that he might redeem us from all iniquity, and purify unto himself a peculiar people, zealous of good works."* This is a text to which we often refer, as describing the essence of the Christian religion; and conveying, in the clearest manner, our belief in the quality, the universality, and the effects of that gift of Divine Grace, to which the apostle bears this ample testimony; and which we here see, co-operates with that great object, for which the Son of God was manifested in the flesh. This object, according to the testimony of another apostle, was, "To destroy the works of the devil;"† the principal of which, it scarcely need be said, is sin.

But to return to the preceding passage in Titus. There are three inferences evidently resulting from it. 1.—That this Grace is of that quality, which produceth salvation. 2.— That it is universal : not confined to a part of mankind ; but extended "to all men." 3.—That its instructions are such as invariably lead to the practice of piety and virtue. The first and third of these inferences will, it is presumed, be generally, if not universally acceded to ; but the second, though equally deducible from the

* Titus ii. 11.—14.   † 1 John iii. 8.

apostle's words, some may endeavour to explain away; and to reconcile with those ideas of unconditional election and reprobation, which they have entertained; and on which it may be proper, in this place, to make a few remarks.

This doctrine asserts, that the Almighty has irrevocably decreed a certain number of human beings to everlasting happiness; and that the rest are as certainly doomed to the commission of sin, and to its consequence, eternal misery. That this is no exaggerated description, will appear from the quotations given in the margin,* from the writings of the advocates of this doctrine; and I should think, that to describe it, was enough to refute it, had we not, in many other instances, as well as in this, occasion to

* " I say, that by the ordination and will of God, Adam fell. God would have man to fall. We refer the cause of hardening us to God."—*Calvin.* " God hath predestinated not only unto damnation, but also unto the causes of it, whomsoever he saw meet."—*Beza.* " It is the opinion of our doctrines, that God did inevitably decree the temptation and fall of man."— *Parœus.* " God moveth the robber to kill. He killeth, God forcing him thereunto."—*Zuinglius.* " Reprobate persons," saith *Piscator,* " are absolutely ordained to this two-fold end; to undergo everlasting punishment, and necessarily to sin; and therefore to sin, that they may be justly punished."—See Barclay's Apology, prop. v. sect. 2.

observe, in how different a point of view different men see the same subject. That the Holy Scriptures, those faithful records both of the justice and mercy of God, should be pressed to the support of such a sentiment, is matter of surprise. I am aware that some parts of the Scriptures, taken without their context, may be supposed to incline to this sentiment.* This is particularly the case in the Epistle to the Romans, in which the apostle is setting forth the call of the Gentiles, and the temporary rejection of the Jews; justifying, with great energy, the power and the wisdom, the goodness and the severity of God, in this respect: but that he meant thereby to inculcate, that the Almighty, personally and unconditionally, elect—

* It is worthy of remark, that several passages in our English translation, which seem to favour this doctrine, are capable of a different rendering. For instance, in Acts ii. 23, where it is translated, " Him being delivered by the determinate counsel and foreknowledge of God," &c. the Greek word, ἔκδοτον, rendered *delivered*, may, with equal, or more propriety, be translated, *given forth* : then the passage may be read thus : " Him, who was given forth by the determinate counsel and foreknowledge of God, ye have taken, and with wicked hands have crucified and slain." Another Greek word is used in every passage that is rendered, *delivered*. Acts iv. 27. and 1 Peter ii. 8. are also capable of being differently translated.

ed individuals to a state of future happiness, and decreed others to a state of misery, is what, I think, no fair construction of the Epistle will warrant. On the contrary, after showing and enforcing the right of the Almighty, to make use of individuals, or of nations, for carrying on his great and unsearchable designs ; the apostle sets forth, even with respect to the Gentiles, the call of whom it was peculiarly his object to justify, that their continuance in divine favour, depended upon the steadfastness of their faith and faithfulness to Him, who had "called them out of darkness into his marvellous light";* and "made them partakers of his promise in Christ Jesus."†

The following quotation from that part of the epistle in which the apostle may be said to sum up his arguments, will tend to set the subject in a clear light: "For I speak to you Gentiles; inasmuch as I am the apostle of the Gentiles, I magnify mine office.—If some of the branches be broken off, and thou, being a wild olive tree, wert graffed in among them; and with them partakest of the root and fatness of the olive tree, boast not against the branches; but if thou boast [remember] thou bearest not

* 1 Pet. ii. 9.   † Ephes. iii. 6.

the root, but the root thee.   Thou wilt say then, the branches were broken off, that I might be graffed in.   Well, because of unbelief they were broken off, and thou standest by faith; be not high minded, but fear; for if God spared not the natural branches, take heed lest he also spare not thee.   Behold therefore the goodness and severity of God, on them which fell, severity; but towards thee, goodness, if thou continue in his goodness; otherwise thou also shalt be cut off: and they also, if they abide not still in unbelief, shall be graffed in; for God is able to graff them in again."*

Here we see no unconditional election or reprobation; but a doctrine which perfectly comports with the declaration of the Almighty about six hundred years before, when, after sending the prophet Jeremiah to the potter's house, to instruct him at once in the Divine power and mercy, he sent a message by him to the house of Israel, in this memorable language: " O House of Israel! Cannot I do with you as this potter, saith the Lord? Behold, as the clay is in the potter's hand, so are ye in my hand, O house of Israel!"† After thus setting forth his

* Rom. xi. 13—23.   † Jer. xviii. 6.

power, the Almighty proceeds to show in what manner He is pleased to exercise it : " At what instant I shall speak concerning a nation and concerning a kingdom, to pluck up, and to pull down, and to destroy it ; if that nation, against which I have pronounced, turn from their evil, I will repent of the evil that I thought to do unto them. And at what instant I shall speak concerning a nation, and concerning a kingdom, to build and to plant it : if it do evil in my sight, that it obey not my voice, then I will repent of the good, wherewith I said I would benefit them."*

Thus we see the principle of the dealings of God, with mankind, in different ages of the world. The Ninevites are a proof of the truth of the first part of the foregoing declaration ; and the Israelites of the latter : for, however, the Almighty may, in some instances, see meet to distinguish a people, or individuals, by some peculiar privileges ; yet if they neglect, and trample upon his law ; and are unmindful of the favours which they receive ; he does not fail to punish them accordingly : " You only have I known of all the families of the earth ; therefore I will punish you for all your iniquities,"†

* Jer. xviii. 7, 10.　　† Amos iii. 2.

was the declaration concerning this highly favoured people; from which, and various other
passages in holy writ, we may safely conclude,
that man's destruction is of himself; agreeably
to another declaration of the Almighty by one
of his prophets: "O Israel! thou hast destroyed
thyself; but in me is thine help."† "The grace
of God which bringeth salvation, and hath appeared unto all men," affordeth this help. It
is saving grace; and it is universal grace. It is
a gift consistent with every attribute of the
Deity; and with the declarations concerning
Him, recorded in the Scriptures of Truth.

That the Almighty may see meet, in his unsearchable wisdom, to confer a greater degree of this
grace on some than on others; and that he may
peculiarly call some to particular services in his
church, or in the world, are no doubt consistent with the Divine attributes: but with respect
to the future happiness of mankind, there is
abundant reason to believe, that all receive a
sufficient degree of grace to procure it; and if
this grace is not equally distributed to all, yet,
surely, we may conclude that, at last, the judgment will be according to this most excellent rule:
"Where much is given much will be required;"‡

† Hosea xiii. 9.   ‡ Luke xii. 48.

and, consequently, that where little is given but little will be required.

In addition to what has already been said, it may be proper to observe, that, in considering this subject, we should always distinguish between those passages in the Scriptures, which simply declare the power of the Almighty, and those which set forth the manner in which he exercises that power. Thus the apostle has said, and no doubt said truly: "He hath mercy on whom he will have mercy; and whom he will he hardeneth."* But then are we not also told that, "the Lord is good to all; and his tender mercies are over all his works;"† and has not the very same apostle, after recommending that, "prayers and intercessions should be made for all men,"‡ expressly declared, that "this is good and acceptable in the sight of God our Saviour, who will have all men to be saved, and to come unto the knowledge of the truth?"§ Correspondent with this is the language of the apostle Peter: "The Lord is not slack concerning his promise, as some men count slackness, but is long suffering to us-ward; not wil-

* Rom. ix. 18.   † Psalm cxlv. 9.   ‡ 1 Tim. ii. 1.
§ 1 Tim. ii. 3, 4.

ling that any should perish, but that all should come to repentance."*

It should also be considered, that hardness of heart is the punishment, and not the original cause, of sin ; nor does the hardness spoken of by the apostle in the Epistle to the Romans, necessarily imply perpetual hardness ; for of the Jews whom he represents in a state of hardness, he says : "If they abide not still in unbelief, they shall be graffed in again."†

If God did judicially harden or suffer to be hardened, those who had been long wilfully disobedient to his laws, he might, with great propriety, "show his wrath, and make his power known in the vessels of wrath, fitted for destruction"‡ by their own accumulated transgressions. Thus were Pharaoh and the Jews monuments of the justice of an offended God, and warnings to succeeding generations, not to despise those long suffering mercies, with which He waits the return of those who sin against him.

Seeing then that the designs of our great and gracious Creator are so replete with "good-will

* 2 Peter iii. 9.　　† Rom. xi. 23.　　‡ Ib. ix. 22.

to men;" that, as far as is consistent with the free agency, with which he has seen meet to endow us, He is ever willing our happiness, and furnishing us with the means of procuring it; "Let us draw nigh with a true heart, in full assurance of faith;"* and, trusting in that merciful redemption, by which we have, on repentance, the forgiveness of sins, "Let us come boldly to the throne of grace, that we may obtain mercy, and find grace to help in time of need."† Thus will that sanctification of heart, and holiness of life, be experienced, without which, we are told: "No man shall see the Lord;"‡ and thus all will redound to the glory of God, who has "shown the exceeding riches of his grace, in his kindness towards us, through Christ Jesus."§

* Heb. x. 22. † Ibid. iv. 16, ‡ Ibid. xii. 14.
§ Ephes. ii. 7.

CHAP. V.

ON DIVINE WORSHIP AND GOSPEL MINISTRY.

Worship an act of the soul towards God.—Meetings for worship may be held in silence.—Public worship an indispensable duty—reasonable and beneficial.—Silent worship adapted to all states.—Its advantages.—Scripture arguments for it.—Prayer a necessary duty.—The qualifications of Ministers.—Human learning not essential to the Ministry—No individual has a right exclusively to assume the exercise of it.—On Women's preaching.— On preaching for hire.—Tithes.

HAVING, in the preceding chapters treated on those subjects in which we nearly agree with the generality of Christian professors, I come now to consider those points, in which we materially differ from them. Two of these, being nearly connected, are included in one chapter, though it will also be necessary to consider them separately. These are, Divine Worship and Gospel Ministry.

With respect to the first, we consider that worship is an act of the soul towards God ; that

He is a Spirit; that the soul of man is spiritual; and therefore that, in the performance of the solemn duty of worship, words are not essen- tially necessary; because He, who is a Spirit, understands the language of the Spirit. Never- theless, we do not disapprove the use of words in our religious meetings, whether in prayer, praises, or in the exercise of gospel ministry; when they are delivered under the influence of the Holy Spirit, which only can, as we appre- hend, rightly qualify for the performance of these important services. Hence, when we come to our places of religious worship, we think it right to sit down in silence, and wait therein upon God, for the assistance of that Spirit which helpeth our infirmities, and with- out which we know not what to pray for as we ought. Here we may be favoured, at times, to feel the Spirit itself making intercession for us; under the influence of which, we believe, a se- cret aspiration will ascend with more accep- tance before the Father of spirits, than any form of words which may be prepared for us, or that does not arise from a heart thus quali- fied for verbal expression.

Holding our meetings under these impres- sions, it very frequently happens that they are continued throughout in silence; a state which when attended with a right exercise of mind, we consider as best adapted to the performance of the solemn duty of divine worship: for here, every individual who feels his own condition and necessities, can secretly pour out his soul unto God, without distraction or interruption; and here also we can freely partake of those Divine influences upon the mind, which, when mercifully afforded, constitute the highest enjoyment of man upon earth.

But we are sensible that these effects are not always experienced in our religious meetings. We fear that some who attend them, have not their minds rightly exercised; we know that Divine good is not at our command: and we believe that the sensible enjoyment of it, is often withheld for a season, and sometimes for a long season, from the truly exercised mind: " Verily thou art a God that hidest thyself, O God of Israel, the Saviour!"* But, even in this situation, we think it much safer to wait in a state of passive silence, than, by the activity of the creature, to rush unprepared into those external acts of devotion, which we believe are no fur-

* Isaiah xlv. 15.

ther acceptable, than as they come from a heart rightly prepared to offer them. A state of humble, silent waiting, and dependance on Divine help, is so adapted to the relation in which man stands to his great Creator, that we believe it peculiarly likely to meet with Divine acceptance and regard: " Blessed are those servants, whom the Lord, when he cometh, shall find watching."* But to those who do not patiently abide in this state of mind, a very different consequence is shown to result: " Behold, all ye that kindle a fire, that compass yourselves about with sparks: walk in the light of your fire, and in the sparks that ye have kindled. This shall ye have of mine hand; ye shall lie down in sorrow."† And we ought by no means to forget the consequence, under the law, of offering strange fire to the Lord.‡

We consider it an indispensable duty, publicly to meet together for the worship of God; and " not to forsake the assembling of ourselves together, as the manner of some is."§ It is both a reasonable and a beneficial duty; reasonable, because it is a public acknowledgment of our

* Luke xii. 37.   † Is. l. 11.   ‡ Lev. x. 1 to 5.
§ Heb. x. 25.

E

dependance on the Supreme Being; and beneficial, because we may, if rightly exercised in
our minds, be favoured to draw nigh unto God,
by the Spirit of his Son; and thus experience
that communion, which is with the Father and
with his Son Christ Jesus; and which the true
Christian travellers also have one with another,
in Him.

In a silent travail of spirit for this desirable
experience, the spiritual strength of those who
are thus exercised, is increased; they become
helpful one to another, in promoting the circula-
tion of that life in which their fellowship con-
sists; and are, at times, so united in feeling one
for and with another, as to attain to an experience, similar to that which the apostle describes:
" Whether one member suffer, all the members
suffer with it; or one member be honoured, all
the members rejoice with it."*

It may be supposed by some, that although
this mode of worship may be adapted to adults
in religious experience, it is too refined an at-
tainment for those who are in a state of infancy
in religion; or who are much strangers to it.—
We, however, consider it as eminently adapted

* 1 Cor. xii. 26.

to every human being, who is desirous of being acceptable in the sight of his Creator. Where is the well disposed mind, that has not occasion for an attention to that universal command: "What I say unto you, I say unto all, Watch!"* This secret attention and exercise of mind, is therefore necessary for all; and as man is willing to be reduced into it, the weak and erring mind may be brought to the discovery of its own state; and, feeling the necessity of Divine aid, to overcome its evil propensities, and to secure eternal happiness, may thus feel also the necessity and the qualification, to pray for forgiveness of past sins, and for ability so to live under the influences of Divine fear and love, as to experience preservation from those evils which abound in the world, or to which the mind may be naturally prone.

Many, therefore, we conceive, are the advantages which result from silent worship. It enables a number of Christians to meet together for the performance of this important duty, without depending on any man to assist them therein; a dependance, which deprives numbers of publicly discharging this duty, even once in

* Mark xiii. 37.

the week. It also preserves from the dangerous situation, of drawing nigh unto God with the mouth, and honouring him with the lips, whilst the heart is far from Him; and it is peculiarly adapted to the performance of that worship in spirit and in truth, concerning which our blessed. Redeemer has given this memorable testimony: "The hour cometh, and now is, when the true worshippers shall worship the Father, in spirit and in truth; for the Father seeketh such to worship him. God is a Spirit; and they that worship Him, must worship Him in spirit and in truth."*

In addition to the foregoing reasons, many passages may be adduced from the Scriptures, pointing out the advantage of silent waiting upon God. In reading those devotional effusions, which have been transmitted to us in the book of Psalms, we find this waiting strongly and frequently inculcated. The evangelical prophet likewise speaks frequently of the benefit of such a state of waiting, in which silence is either expressed, or necessarily implied. The latter part of the fortieth chapter, and the beginning of the forty-first, are so apposite to the

* John iv. 23 and 24.

present subject; and at the same time, so replete
with religious instruction and consolation, that
it may be useful to give them at large : " Why
sayest thou, O Jacob, and speakest, O Israel ?
My way is hid from the Lord, and my judgment
is passed over from my God ? Hast thou not
known ? hast thou not heard, that the everlasting
God, the Lord, the Creator of the ends of the
earth, fainteth not, neither is weary ?   There is
no searching of his understanding. He giveth
power to the faint, and to them that have no
might, he increaseth strength. Even the youths-
shall faint and be weary, and the young men
utterly fall : but they that wait upon the Lord
shall renew their strength; they shall mount up
with wings as eagles ; they shall run and not
be weary ; they shall walk and not faint. Keep
silence before me, O islands ; and let the people renew their strength ; let them come near,
then let them speak ; let us come near together
to judgment."*

But whilst we are laying aside the outward
forms, we are far, very far indeed, from desiring to discourage the practice of true prayer.
It is a duty which we owe to our great Creator ;
and which the feelings of our own manifold

* Isaiah xl. 27 to 31. and xli. 1.

E 3

wants and dangers, will often draw from the
rightly concerned mind. It is indeed difficult
to conceive, how any thing deserving the name
of religion, can be preserved without it.—
" Watch and pray, that ye enter not into temptation,"* is an injunction delivered by our
Holy Head and High Priest, who in this, as in
many other instances, has shown, that he was,
as the author of the Epistle to the Hebrews
expresses it, " Touched with the feeling of our
infirmities;"† for he immediately adds: " the
Spirit indeed is willing; but the flesh is weak."

In this command, our blessed Lord sets forth
both the necessity and the preparation for this
great duty, which constitutes a very important
part of religious worship. We are not to rush
hastily or unpreparedly either into private or
public prayer; but having our minds engaged
in true watchfulness, or waiting for the influence of the Holy Spirit upon the soul, we
thereby become qualified to put up our petitions
to the Father of Spirits in such a manner as
the impressions which he affords us of our wants
shall indicate. And when we are brought into
a humbling consideration, of the many mercies
and favours, of which we are unworthy par-

* Matt. xxvi. 41.   † Heb. iv. 15.

takers, as the objects of creation, of redemption, and of that bountiful provision which is made for us, we shall find abundant cause frequently to offer that praise, by which the Almighty is glorified ; and of which he is, with the Son of his love, through the eternal Spirit, for ever worthy.

After these remarks on religious worship, we proceed to the consideration of the subject of Gospel Ministry.

The right qualification of those who occupy the station of ministers, is of great importance to every religious society. It will, I presume, be universally agreed to be, in the first place, necessary that the principles and practice of these, should correspond with their profession and station ; and next, that they be called and qualified, according to the nature and principles of that religion, which they stand forth to espouse. To apply these self-evident rules to the Christian religion, under its various divi- sions, it must be deemed necessary for a gospel minister, that he possess a heartfelt conviction of the truths of Christianity, as well as of the principles of that particular society, of which he is a member ; also that his moral conduct be such as the gospel of Christ requires. When there is any material deficiency either in principle or practice, there is reason to fear that such will do more injury than benefit to the cause of religion; as well as render themselves objects of disgust and contempt. "Unto the wicked, God saith, what hast thou to do to declare my statutes; or that thou shouldst take my covenant in thy mouth; seeing thou hatest instruction, and castest my words behind thee?"*

As to the further qualification for a gospel minister, although the definition already given may be generally agreed to, yet, in the application of it, there exists some diversity of sentiment. As the nature and principles of the Christian religion, are the same now as formerly, we conceive that the same Divine call and influence, which qualified the early ministers and promulgators of the gospel, should be, in a degree at least, experienced by its ministers to the end of the world: especially as we have no other qualification pointed out in the Holy Scriptures. This call was "not of men, neither by man; but by Jesus Christ, and God, the Father."† We believe that the same is inwardly and immediately received, by the true

* Psalm l. 16 and 17.　　　† Gal. i. l.

gospel ministers of the present day; and that, in the discharge of the duties of this sacred office, the renewed influences of Divine wisdom and strength, should be waited for and experienced. Thus ministers are qualified to speak to the state of their hearers; and to baptize them into the name [or power] of the Father, the Son, and the Holy Spirit ; thereby fulfilling that true commission for gospel ministry, given by our Saviour, Matt. xxviii. 19.

The foregoing qualifications correspond with the description, which the apostle Peter gives of prophecy, and which we conceive to be descriptive of the essentials of a gospel minister. " Prophecy came not in old time by the will of man: but holy men of God spake as they were moved by the Holy Ghost."* Thus we see, that both ancient prophecy and gospel ministry, came " not of men, nor by man;" that they required those who exercised them to be holy men of God; such as could say to others: " Walk, as ye have us for an example;†" and that in performing the duties of these offices, they should speak " as they were moved by the Holy Ghost ;" or in other words, as the " Spirit

* 2. Peter i. 21. † Phil. iii. 17.

L 5

gave them utterance."* If ministers are not thus influenced and directed, we may expect the declaration respecting the prophets formerly, who ran and were not sent, to be verified: "They shall not profit the people at all."† Nor should this serious language be forgotten: "Wo unto the foolish prophets, that follow their own spirit, and have seen nothing,"‡

What is said respecting an inward call to the ministry, is by no means peculiar to our religious society. However the doctrine of the influence of the Spirit may be slighted by some, it is in this instance, as well as in its general influence and operation, clearly maintained by the church of England, as appears by the following question put to those who apply to be admitted to the office of deacon: "Do you trust that you are *inwardly moved by the Holy Ghost*, to take upon you this office and ministration," &c. The answer required is, "I trust so." This doctrine is also consistent with the general observation on the priesthood, made by the author of the Epistle to the Hebrews: "No man taketh this honour unto himself, but he that is called of God, as was Aaron."§ The writ-

* Acts ii. 4.   † Jer. xxiii. 32.   ‡ Ezek. xiii. 3.
§ Heb. v. 4.

ings of the apostles abundantly show, not only whence they derived their commission, but also the influence under which they exercised it. Thus the Apostle Paul says : " Which things also we speak, not in the words which man's wisdom teacheth, but which the Holy Ghost teacheth."*

From all these considerations, we believe, as is already stated, that it is necessary, in the first call to the ministry, to be " inwardly moved by the Holy Ghost;" and that, in the various performances of this sacred office, the renewings of this Divine influence and ability, should be waited for and experienced, as the most likely means to fulfil the apostolic exhortation : " If any man speak, let him speak as the oracles of God ; if any man minister, let him do it as of the ability which God giveth ; that God in all things may be glorified through Jesus Christ ; to whom be praise and dominion for ever and ever. Amen."†

From our views of this important subject, there arise a few points, in which we materially differ from most other professors of Christianity.

* 1 Cor. ii. 13.   † 1 Peter iv. 11.

1.—In not considering human learning essential to a gospel minister.

2.—In believing that no individual has a right, to assume the exclusive exercise of this ministry, in a congregation of Christians; but that all, both male and female, who are rightly moved thereto, may exercise this gift.

3.—That this ministry being, if rightly received, received freely, and without any pecuniary expense to qualify for it, it therefore ought to be freely communicated; and no further support expected by ministers, than what is authorized by Christ, and was practised by his apostles.

Upon each of these points it seems proper to make a few remarks.

On the first very little appears necessary; for if we consider the holy scriptures, and particularly the New Testament, as any guide to us in this matter, we shall not only find, that human literature is no where recommended for this office; but likewise, that many of the apostles were illiterate men. It is also clear that the apostle Paul, though a man of learning, disclaimed the influence of it upon his ministry, as appears from various parts of his epistles, particularly from the first and second chapters of the epistle to the Corinthians, of which the first five verses of the second chapter, appear especially worthy of notice: "And I, brethren, when I came to you, came not with excellency of speech or of wisdom, declaring unto you the testimony of God: for I determined not to know any thing among you, save Jesus Christ, and him crucified. And I was with you in weakness, and in fear, and in much trembling: and my speech and my preaching was not with enticing words of man's wisdom, but in demonstration of the Spirit and of power: that your faith should not stand in the wisdom of men, but in the power of God."*

But although we do not consider human learning as essential to a gospel minister; yet we are so far from disesteeming or slighting its use, that we wish due attention to be paid to it by the members of our society: for we believe that those who have it, and are disposed to make a right use of it, may apply it to the promotion

* 1 Cor. ii. 1 to 5.

of religion and virtue, as well as to the benefit of civil society.

With respect to the second point, we have the practice of the primitive church so decidedly in our favour, that I am at a loss to conceive how a practice so repugnant to it, can have so generally prevailed as it has done, in almost all the Christian churches.

The practice alluded to is that of an individual assuming the exclusive exercise of the ministry ; which is directly contrary to what the apostle recommends, as well as declares to be the practice of the church in early times. This appears clear from the fourteenth chapter of the first epistle to the Corinthians, where, first addressing the believers in general, the apostle thus expresses himself : " Follow after charity, and desire spiritual gifts ; but rather that ye may prophesy."* By this prophesying, he does not appear so much to mean the fortelling of future events, as the general purposes of gospel ministry ; for in the third verse he says : " He that prophesieth, speaketh unto men to edification, and exhortation, and comfort."† After this general advice and explanation, he proceeds to

* 1 Cor. xiv, 1.   † 1 Cor. xiv. 3.

show the superiority of prophesying to speaking with tongues; and then, of those who have received this divine gift, he says, " Let the prophets speak two or three, and let the others judge. If any thing be revealed to another that sitteth by, let the first hold his peace; for ye may all prophecy one by one, that all may learn, and all may be comforted."*

After stating this unequivocal description of the rule and practice of the primitive church, I shall proceed to the consideration of another part of this head, from which it appears that we admit women, as well as men, to a participation and exercise of the gift of gospel ministry. We are aware of the objection which is made, from the prohibition laid upon women speaking and teaching in the church, and usurping authority over the man.† But if, on every occasion, where there is an apparent difference between one part of scripture and another, it is admitted that scripture is the best interpreter of scripture, I believe very little difficulty will arise in removing this objection. It should be considered, that the words used by the apostle on this occasion, cannot mean the exercise of gos-

* 1 Cor. xiv. 29 to 31.　　† 1 Tim. ii. 11—15.

pel ministry; because in the very epistle in which he first mentions this prohibition, he gives particular directions respecting the manner in which women are to exercise that gift, which he denominates, "praying or prophesying;"* and which he no doubt considered as different from speaking, teaching, or usurping authority : for it cannot with any colour of reason be supposed, that the apostle would give directions for the exercise of that, which he thought should never be exercised."†

In addition to the preceding argument, several other passages in the Old and New Testaments may be advanced, which clearly show, that women, as well as men, were engaged in the work of the ministry, or as prophetesses in early times. Passing over Miriam, Deborah, and Huldah, we find Anna, a prophetess in the Jewish Church, publicly exercising her gift in the Temple; and hailing the recent birth of the Messiah. The Samaritan woman, with whom our Saviour held an interesting conversation at Jacob's Well, appears to have been the first of his disciples, who publicly preached the coming

* 1 Cor. xi. 4.

See John Locke's note on Cor. xi. 3. where he supports the construction here given.

of Christ; and remarkable was the success which attended her ministry. Women were the first witnesses of our Lord's resurrection, and were commissioned by him to proclaim this important truth to his disciples.

After his ascension, they were, equally with the men, partakers of the effusions of the Holy Spirit; and we find several females mentioned as being prophetesses or fellow-labourers with the apostles in the Gospel of Christ. Luke, in speaking of Philip the deacon, says : "the same man had four daughters, which did prophesy."* In the Epistle to the Romans, the apostle says : "I recommend unto you Phebe our sister, who is a servant of the church that is at Cenchrea."†a— Greet Priscilla b and Aquila, my helpers in Christ Jesus."‡ " Salute Tryphæna and Tryphosa, who labour in the Lord. Salute the

* Acts xxi. 9.

a The Greek word in this passage rendered servant, is the same as in other places is rendered deacon or minister. It is rendered minister here in almost all other translations.

b Priscilla is here, and in two other passages, placed before her husband; from which, and other circumstances, we may conclude she was a minister of no small eminence in the church.

† Rom. xvi. 1. ‡ Rom. xvi. 3.

beloved Persis, *c* which laboured much d in the Lord."*   And in another epistle he says, " Help those women that laboured with us in the gospel."†

These are passages which clearly evince the admission of the female sex, in early times, to the work and service of the gospel : but what adds not a little to our argument is, that this was expressly foretold in such a manner, as would, if we had no precedent, fully warrant the practice: for on this subject we may use the words of the apostle Peter, and say : " This is that which was spoken by the prophet Joel: And it shall come to pass in the last days, saith God, I will pour out of my Spirit upon all flesh, and your sons and your *daughters* shall prophesy; and your young men shall see visions, and your old men shall dream dreams: and on my servants, and on my *handmaidens*, I will pour out in those days of my Spirit, and they shall prophesy."‡

c The adjective for " beloved," being in Greek in the feminine gender, shows that Persis was a woman.

d The Greek words here rendered " labour and laboured are the same as the apostle uses when he speaks of himself labouring in the gospel.

* Rom. xvi. 12,   † Phil. iv. 3.
‡ Acts ii. 16 to 18.

We come now to the third point, viz. the maintenance which is allowed to the ministers of the Gospel. On this subject the directions of our blessed Lord are so particular, that, with the practice of his Apostles, they set the matter in a very clear point of view. The directions, so far as they relate to this subject, I shall transcribe from the tenth chapter of Matthew, when Christ sent forth the twelve Apostles on their first mission: " Heal the sick, cleanse the lepers, raise the dead, cast out devils: freely ye have received, freely give. Provide neither gold, nor silver, nor brass in your purses :—for the workman is worthy of his meat. And into whatsoever city or town ye shall enter, inquire who in it is worthy, and therein abide till ye go thence. And whosoever shall not receive you, nor hear your words, when ye depart out of that house or city, shake off the dust of your feet."*

In the foregoing passage, we have directions for the conduct of the ministers of Christ, both when their ministry is received, and when it is rejected. In the former case, all that is provided is temporary accommodation, whilst travelling in the work of the ministry; or so en-

* Matt. x. 8 to 14.

gaged therein, as to prevent their attention to
their temporal occupations.   In the latter case,
they are by no means authorized to extort a
forced maintenance ; but, as a testimony against
those who reject them, they are directed to
shake off the dust that cleaved to their feet.
Well would it have been for the Christian religion, had its ministers, under all denominations,
adhered to their Lord's instructions on this subject ; and acted with that noble disinterestedness which he inculcates, and which we find
practised by his immediate followers, so as to
enable one of them to say, "I seek not your's
but you."*

And here I cannot well avoid expressing great regret for the wound, which, there
is reason to believe, Christianity has received,
and still receives, from a lucrative establishment
for ministers ; a circumstance which holds out
a temptation for unqualified, and even immoral
men, to seek for, and get into that office, with
no better motive (I believe it will be generally
allowed) than that which it was foretold would
actuate the corrupted sons of Eli : "Put me, I
pray thee, into one of the priest's offices, that I
may eat a piece of bread."†

* 2 Cor. xii. 14.   † 1 Sam. ii. 36.

We are aware of the arguments advanced from some expressions of the apostle Paul, in favour of an established support for ministers; and which I apprehend are all comprised in the following words of the Apostle: "Do ye not know, that they which minister about holy things, live of the things of the temple; and they which wait at the altar, are partakers with the altar? Even so hath the Lord ordained, that they which preach the Gospel, should live of the Gospel."* Now all this only proves a support consistent with what "the Lord hath ordained," and which is already given in his own words. This we readily admit, and adopt in our practice; but surely no one can infer, from the foregoing passages, that ministers are to be provided with a settled maintenance; and not to labour with their hands, or to be engaged in the usual occupations of life for their own support, and that of their families.

That we are justified in the construction given of our Lord's direction, and the Apostle's reference to it, is abundantly clear from the practice which resulted from it; and which cannot more completely or energetically be described, than in the words of the same Apostle,

* 1 Cor. ix. 13, 14.

contained in his most excellent address to the elders of Ephesus, which he concludes in this memorable language: "I have coveted no man's silver, or gold, or apparel; yea, you yourselves know that these hands have ministered unto my necessities, and to them that were with me. I have showed you all things, how that so labouring, ye ought to support the weak, and to remember the words of the Lord Jesus, how he said, It is more blessed to give than to receive."*

These being our sentiments on this important subject, we make no provision for the support of our ministers, further than the discharge of those expenses, which travelling in their religious services necessarily occasions; and if we make no provision for the support of our own ministers, whose ministry we approve, we think ourselves fully warranted in declining to contribute to the support of others, and of a worship connected with them, from both of which we conscientiously dissent.   A ministry with a settled maintenance, forced even from those, who so far disapprove of their establishment, as to withdraw from their teaching, is so evidently incompatible with the doctrine and

* Acts xx. 33 to 35.

practice of Christ and his Apostles, that I think it unnecessary to say more to justify our principles in this respect. But although it appears to me to be a system so deeply injurious, to the interests of true religion, I have no doubt that many, not seeing the subject in the same point of view, have seriously entered, under these circumstances, into this vocation; and are piously concerned to discharge the duties of their station. These should be left to their own master, to whom we must all, at last, either stand or fall.

After what has been said respecting the general maintenance of Gospel Ministers, it appears superfluous to enter into argument against that most objectionable and anti-christian mode, of support by tithes. Their divine right is generally exploded and abandoned; their impolicy is almost as universally acknowledged. How far the testimony which we have borne against them may have contributed to produce these effects, is not for me to determine; but it is hoped that so long as this yoke remains, that testimony will continue to be maintained, with the firmness and meekness which should ever be united in the support of religious truths.

CHAP. VI.

ON BAPTISM AND THE SUPPER.

Preliminary Observations.—Two Kinds of Baptism— Water and the Spirit:—Remarks on Matt. xxviii. 19.— This and other Arguments in favour of Water Baptism answered. — Sprinkling not Baptism. — Sprinkling of Infants not authorized by Scripture. — Circumstances attending it highly objectionable.—The Lord's Supper.— The Circumstances attending it fully admitted.—Not considered perpetual, any more than washing of Feet.— The true Lord's Supper.— Our Dissent on these Subjects, not from Disesteem of Christianity, but the reverse.

BEFORE entering into a separate consideration of these subjects, I shall premise a few words on the nature of religious observances and ceremonies. These appear to me to be generally local or temporary; and, if we may judge from what we read in the New Testament, we may safely conclude, that the use of them is variable. There is not a practice more strictly enjoined by our blessed Lord, and that both by precept and example, than the washing of each other's feet, as related by th evangelist John. chap. xiii. But who, consider-, ing the different local circumstances, believes this to be a duty now incumbent upon us ? The apostles who met at Jerusalem, to consider the attempt of some Jewish Christians. to im- pose the rite of circumcision on those Gentiles who embrace Christianity, came to a solemn, and no doubt, right conclusion on such things, as it was then deemed necessary to observe ;* yet none of these, except one of a moral nature, is now considered obligatory. Nay, we even find the apostle Paul, a few years after, en- forcing a liberty with respect to meats offered to idols, which this decree certainly does not warrant; a decree which there is great reason to believe he had himself united in forming.

The Christian church was at that time, just emerging from the ceremonies of Judaism, and the superstitions of Heathenism. In this state of things, " it seemed good to the Holy Ghost," gradually to remove those legal observances and ceremonies, connected with the Mosaic dispensation; and not to enjoin an immediate disregard, to the whole of them at once. It was the morning of the gospel

* Acts xv.

P

day; and if the brightness of that morning has been greatly obscured, which I apprehend all protestants agree with us in believing; and that the sun has been prevented from shining forth with meridian splendour, by the darkness of many unnecessary observances and traditions, which were afterwards introduced into the Christian church; we must indeed regret the circumstance: but when further light is renewed and afforded, ought we not to avail ourselves of its advantages, and endeavour to stand open to those further discoveries, which are consistent with the nature and spirit of the gospel; and which may be supported as such, by the doctrines contained in the Holy Scriptures, particularly in the New Testament?

After making these general remarks, we may proceed to the consideration of the subject of Baptism. Of this we find two kinds mentioned in the New Testament; namely, Baptism with Water, and Baptism with the Spirit. The former was, in some degree, in use under the Jewish law; and some writers mention that it was occasionally both added to circumcision, and substituted for it, in the admission of proselytes. When the forerunner of our Lord appeared, to fulfil his mission, he made particular use of this ceremony; and from him it was called the Baptism of John. From this practice among the Jews, and by John the baptist, Water Baptism appears to have been introduced into the Christian church, as the mode of acknowledging its converts; but we conceive it was no more an essential part of Christianity, than other Jewish ceremonies, for a time practised by the early Christians.

It is clear that John considered his dispensation and baptism as only temporary; nor does he, as a substitute for his baptism, refer his disciples to any other baptism with water, to be instituted by Christ. On the contrary, he plainly shows, that the baptism which was to supersede his, was to be of a different and a spiritual nature, as appears by these words: " I indeed baptize you with water unto repentance; but he that cometh after me is mightier than I, whose shoes I am not worthy to bear: he shall baptize you with the Holy Ghost and with fire; whose fan is in his hand; and he will thoroughly purge his floor, and gather the wheat into his garner; but he will burn up the chaff with unquenchable fire."* On another occasion John also

* Matt. iii. 11 12.

says: " He must increase, but I must decrease."[*] From these expressions, as well as from others in the New Testament, we are induced to believe that the " one Baptism,"[†] which now remains necessary to the church of Christ, is that of the Spirit. This, according to the foregoing instructive allegory, cleanses the heart; and as the apostle Peter informs us, does not consist in putting away the filth of the flesh; but in procuring for us " the answer of a good conscience towards God, by the resurrection of Jesus Christ."[‡]

The practice of Water Baptism is principally defended, by the direction given by our Saviour to his disciples, after his resurrection, when he addressed them in this manner: " Go and teach all nations, baptizing them in the name of the Father, the Son, and the Holy Ghost,"[§] &c. But as we differ from most others in the construction of this passage, it will be proper to enter into a particular consideration of it.

It is to be regretted, that Christians have been so habituated to unite Baptism and Water together in their view, that they seem almost to for-

* John iii. 30.   † Ephes. iv. 5.
‡ 1 Pet. iii. 21.   § Matt. xxviii. 19.

get, that there is a Baptism without Water, by
the Spirit. There are many passages in Scripture, where the words baptize and baptism are
used in a figurative sense, and in which it is evident no allusion to the use of water is intended.
This is peculiarly the case where these words
are used by our blessed Lord, who appears never
to have used them in reference to Water, except
where he expressly so defines the application;
unless it can be intended by the passage in
Matthew now under consideration; and which
we think cannot be proved. There are two instances in which, it is apprehended, all will
agree that Water could not be intended; the
first is the question put to the sons of Zebedee:
" Can ye drink of the cup that I drink of; and
be baptized with the Baptism that I am baptized
with ?"* By these expressions, and similar ones
in the succeeding verse, it is evident that Water
cannot be understood; and, indeed, it is generally agreed, that both the baptism and the cup
allude to a state of deep suffering and afflic-
tion. This is also the obvious meaning of the
expression in Luke : " I have a Baptism to be
baptized with; and how am I straitened till it
be accomplished !"†

* Mark x. 38.　　　† Luke xii. 50.

From these applications of the words baptize and baptism it appears, that they were at that time frequently used in a figurative manner; and we think ourselves warranted in applying the foregoing passage in Matthew, with another in Mark, chap. xvi. 16. to an inward and spiritual Baptism. This construction is much corroborated by rendering the former passage, as the original Greek evidently implies: "Baptizing them *into* the name of the Father," &c. By this expression we apprehend is to be understood, the introducing of the believers into a feeling sense of the power of God in Christ, by the influences of the Holy Spirit; all which the apostles were, no doubt, frequently made instrumental in producing, in the hearts of their hearers. This application of the Word "Name," as symbolical of the Divine power,* is not uncommon in holy writ; and we conceive that no reasonable objection can be made to it. Thus the expressions of our Lord unite with those of the Apostle Paul: "So many as were baptized into Christ Jesus, were baptized into his death:"† and again, "As many as have been baptized into Christ, have put on Christ."‡ That these expressions

* See the Concordances of Cruden and Taylor, under the word, "Name."

† Rom. vi. 3; ‡ Gal. iii. 27.

have no allusion to Water Baptism appears to us evident from the context; and particularly from the following expression of the same apostle: "By one Spirit are we all baptized into one body;—and have been all made to drink into one Spirit."*

It may be alleged, that the apostles under-stood the command in Matthew as applying to Water Baptism, and practised it accordingly. That they made use of baptism with water, has been already admitted ; but that they did it in consequence of this command, is not easy to prove. But supposing this to have been the case, it appears from various circumstances, that even the apostles were "slow of heart to believe" and understand this command, as well as other scriptures relating to the gospel dispensation: for notwithstanding the express charge to " go and teach all nations," connected with the words in dispute, we find how difficult a matter it was, to bring the apostles to this acknowledgment : " Then hath God also to the Gentiles granted repentance unto life."† Such, it is evident, was their attachment to the Jewish nation and law, that they slowly and gradually relinquished many

* 1 Cor. xii. 13.   † Acts xi. 18.

F 4

of those ceremonies which were connected with them; and with some difficulty excused the Gentile converts from an adherence to these observances. The apostle Paul was, however, more quickly introduced into the spirituality of the gospel dispensation; and we think it is clear, that he did not understand our Lord's command, Matt. xxviii. 19. as enjoining the practice of Water Baptism; concerning which it is universally agreed, that he was speaking when he thanked God that he had baptized so very few as he mentions, out of the great numbers converted by him at Corinth to the Christian faith: " For Christ," says he, " sent me not to baptize, but to preach the gospel."*

It has been argued, that this expression of the apostle is general, and only implies that Baptism was not the principal part of his mission. But we have at least an equal right to consider the words in their common acceptation; and as showing that, however the apostle might occasionally use Water Baptism, as a mode of initiating converts into the Christian church, yet he did not consider it as a part of his commission; and consequently not essential to the Christian religion, nor to the soul's salva-

* 1 Cor. i. 17.

tion. If he had considered it necessary to these important objects, it is difficult to conceive how he could solemnly thank God, for the omission of it.

Another argument in favour of Water Baptism is urged from the following query of Peter, on the conversion of Cornelius and his family: "Can any man forbid Water, that these should not be baptized?"* &c. Now it appears very probable from this query, that it was a matter of doubt among the Christians of that time, whether Water Baptism was necessary to be continued; and that Peter on this as well as on some other occasions, inclined to the continuance of a ceremony, at least partly Jewish. How closely even the apostles were attached to the Mosaic law, and how slowly their minds opened to the gospel dispensation, has been already remarked. Notwithstanding the various predictions of the prophets, and the direct command of our Saviour himself after his resurrection, it still required an extraordinary vision from heaven to convince Peter, that, "Of a truth God is no respecter of persons; but in every nation, he that feareth Him, and worketh righteousness, is accepted with

* Acts x. 47.

F 5

Him."* It was about ten years after this circumstance, that the Apostles and Elders came together, to consider of the propriety of exempting the Gentile converts from the rite of circumcision; and it was not till after "there had been much disputing," that they concluded not to impose this yoke upon them. Although Peter was present at this conference, and earnestly promoted the decision of it; yet it was, I apprehend, after this time, that the apostle Paul had occasion to blame him for his changeable conduct towards the Gentiles, with respect to some Jewish customs.† From all these circumstances, we may account for Peter's continuing the practice of Water Baptism, as connected with that dispensation under which he had been educated. However, we have reason to believe that his views on this subject enlarged, as his experience in the service of the gospel increased; for we find him several years after, in one of his epistles, describing the Baptism that "doth now save us"‡ in this manner: "Not the putting away the filth of the flesh; but the answer of a good conscience towards

---

* Acts x. 34 and 35.   † Gal ii. 11, 12, 13.

‡ There appears to be an inaccuracy in our translation of the verse preceding this passage. The "eight souls were saved," not by, but from or through the water; and many translators

God:"* a description by no means applicable
to Water Baptism, which as it was then administered by immersion, did put away the filth
of the flesh ; and of which we may surely say,
as was said of "meats and drinks, and of divers
washings," that it "could not make perfect, as
pertaining to the conscience ;"† they being imposed only until the time of reformation ; by
which is generally understood the gospel dispensation.

In considering the various arguments on this
subject, part of the diversity of sentiment appears
to lie in the difficulty there sometimes is, to determine between the literal and the figurative
use of words, which relate to it. Even water
as well as fire is sometimes used figuratively.
To be "born of *water* and the spirit,"‡ has been
considered, and we think rightly considered, by
‖some who believed in the propriety of Water
Baptism, as figurative an expression, as being
baptized "with the Holy Ghost and with

render it in this sense. Also the Greek word αντιτυπον which
is translated "figure," might be rendered antitype ; a rendering which in this place, gives a different idea of the meaning of
the Apostle.

* 1 Peter iii. 21.

† Heb. ix 9 and 10.   ‡ John iii. 5.

‖ Calvin, Grotious, Piscator, &c.

fire;" and we ought to remember the explanation, which the evangelist himself gives of our
Saviour's use of the word Water: " This
spake he of the Spirit, which they that believed
on him should receive."†

It is frequently said, that Water Baptism is
appointed in the Christian church, as a substitute for Circumcision among the Jews.   In answer to this, I would first query, from what
part of the New Testament can the appoint-
ment of one instead of the other be proved?
Can it be supposed, that if our Saviour, or his
apostles had considered it in this point of view,
they would have given no intimation of it?   I
apprehend that not a single text, which will bear
such a construction, can be produced.   On the
contrary, there are very strong arguments to be
brought against this supposition, from the epistles of the apostle Paul.   He frequently speaks
of circumcision as being no longer of religious
obligation.   If Water Baptism was to have
been its substitute, the occasion to mention it
was almost necessary and unavoidable.   Yet he
is not only silent on the subject of Water Baptism, as the substitute of Circumcision; but he
even shows what is its substitute.   " He is not

* Matt. iii. 11.   † John vii. 39.

a Jew which is one outwardly, neither is that
circumcision which is outward in the flesh; bnt
he is a Jew which is one inwardly; and circumcision is that of the heart, in the spirit, and not
in the letter; whose praise is not of men but of
God."*   In the epistle to the Galatians, the
apostle writes much on the subject of circumcision, but never mentions any other substitute
for it, than " Faith which worketh by love," and
a " new creature."†

What has been said respecting Water Baptism, is intended to apply to it, as it was originally administered by immersion; and in which
manner, I conceive, if it be of religious obligation, it can only be rightly administered.   But
it is a singular fact, that by far the greater number of the advocates for Water Baptism, and
those who are most apt to reflect on us for laying it aside, never practice it themselves; but
have substituted for it the sprinkling of a little
water, in the face of the person pretended to be
baptized; and this they apply to infants more
than to adults.   Now this I think may, with
confidence, be asserted, that Sprinkling is not
Baptism; but if it must have a name of Greek

* Rom. ii. 28 and 29.   † Gal. v. 6. and vi. 15.

derivation, should be called Rantism. Besides, it is a ceremony, which has neither precept nor example in the Holy Scriptures ; the few arguments for it being drawn from equivocal suppositions. For any, therefore, to censure us for the disuse of Water Baptism, who have themselves laid aside the use of it, and substituted something else in its stead, is not a little extraordinary. Which way soever it is administered, it may be an innocent ceremony to those who consider it as a religious duty.

But although the baptizing or sprinkling of Infants may be innocent in itself, there are some circumstances attending its administration, at least in the Church of England, which may be seriously injurious. To say, after a child has passed this ceremony ; " We yield thee hearty thanks, most merciful Father, that it hath pleased thee to regenerate this infant with thy Holy Spirit ; to receive him for thy own child by adoption ; and to incorporate him into thy holy church ;" is saying what, I think, neither reason nor revelation will support ; and if it is seriously believed, must lead those who have passed through the ceremony, when they arrive to years of consideration, to a very mistaken apprehension of their own state.

Another part of this ceremony, and which results from administering it to infants, appears to me to be very objectionable. That which I allude to is, the engagement which those enter into, who become sureties for baptized children. In performing this ceremony, the priest says : " This infant must also faithfully, for his part promise by you that are his sureties, (until he come of age to take it upon himself,) that he will renounce the devil and all his works, and constantly believe God's Holy Word, and obediently keep his commandments. I demand, therefore, Dost thou, in the name of this child, renounce the devil and all his works, the vain pomp and glory of the world, with all covetous desires of the same, and the carnal desires of the flesh, so that thou wilt not follow nor be led by them ? Answer, I renounce them all." Now I appeal to those who are well acquainted with this practice, whether they, who thus engage, do really perform their engagement. Does it clearly appear (as it certainly ought to do) that they always intend it when they make it ? Is their own conduct such as corresponds with the engagement, into which they have entered ? And do they, afterwards, follow up this engagement by means adapted to the end ? Or,

is not this solemn covenant, which is attended
with the most solemn circumstances, often
ightly entered into, and as lightly violated?
Let those who are promoting a practice, in-
volving in it a conduct so repugnant both to
religion and morality, seriously consider what
they are doing; and then I believe they will see
this practice in an awful point of view; and not
be very censorious on us, for laying aside a
ceremony, which, we think, we have good reason to believe, is not an essential part of Christianity; and of which their own practice abundantly convinces us, that the abuse greatly
exceeds the use.

We are, however, sensible that the abuse of
any thing, in itself good and necessary, is not a
sufficient reason for its disuse, nor do we rest
our arguments upon it. It is now left to the
serious consideration of the reader, whether
Water Baptism can be considered as an essential of Christianity, or, whether it may not be
regarded as one of those " divers washings,"
which were imposed for a time only; and
which were gradually to vanish away and cease:
" Christ being come, a High Priest of good
things to come,—by his own blood, entered

once into the holy place, having obtained eternal redemption for us;"* thus, " blotting out the hand-writing of ordinances that was against us, which was contrary to us, he took it out of the way, nailing it to his cross."†

After what has been said on the subject of religious ceremonies in general, and on Baptism in particular, it may not be necessary to add much on what is called the Lord's Supper. We admit that a ceremony, under this name, was in use in the primitive church ; and most probably arose from the circumstances which occurred, when our blessed Lord ate the last passover with his disciples; but we do not think that, thence, an obligation arises upon Christians in general, to retain this ceremony. It was, like Baptism, derived from a Jewish custom ; and when this dispensation was about to be superseded by that of the Gospel, it appears, as has already been observed, that this change was gradual, and the former dispensation not wholly laid aside at once. Admitting therefore, as we do, all the circumstances related on this subject; we cannot conceive, that a recommendation by Christ, to his most intimate

* Heb. ix. 11 and 12.   † Col. ii. 14.

friends and immediate followers, that in future, when they kept the passover, they should have their dear Lord and Master particularly in remembrance, does constitute an obligation upon all those, who should hereafter believe on his name. To desire them to eat that bread and drink that cup in remembrance of him, with this addition, " as oft as ye drink it,"* is, we believe, a very insufficient foundation for the superstructure which has been raised upon it.

It has already been remarked, that the washing of one another's feet, was strongly recommended by our blessed Lord ; and might with at least equal propriety, be now enjoined as a religious obligation on Christians. It may be remembered, that our Lord, having washed the feet of his disciples, afterwards addressed them in this manner : " Know ye what I have done unto you ? Ye call me Master and Lord, and— so I am. If I, then, your Lord and Master, have washed your feet, ye also ought to wash one another's feet : for I have given you an example, that ye should do as I have done to you."† Can any thing so clear, or so positive, be produced in favour of the Lord's Supper, or even of Water Baptism ? Nevertheless, we do

* 1 Cor. xi. 25.   † John xiii. 12 to 15.

not hear of this practice, thus plainly enjoined, being recommended at this day, at least by Protestants, as a Christian duty. And why? Because it is considered, as we consider the others, of a local or temporary nature. If a church, or congregation of Christians, can, in one case, dispense with the use of a religious ceremony, it certainly has the same right to do so in another.

The washing of the feet was a mark of humility, as the supper was of love ; and where the thing signified is felt and acted upon, the emblem might, in our apprehension, be either used or disued, as Christians may consider most conducive to the real advantage of the church. We believe, however, that retaining these ceremonies has, in general, a tendency to settle the minds of the professors of Christianity, in unnecessary forms ; and to prevent their aspiring sufficiently after the practice of real and vital Christianity. The importance attached to this ceremony, we conceive, justifies our apprehensions in this respect; and the abuse which frequently attends its administration, must, we think, in this case, as in that of Baptism, greatly exceed its use. We doubt not the sincerity and piety, with which this ceremony is frequently administered and received; yet we believe, that the true Lord's Supper requires no such elementary mediums as bread and wine for its participation; but that it is the same, and the qualification to receive it the same, as is pointed out by this language to one of the churches: "Behold! I stand at the door, and knock: if any man hear my voice, and open the door, I will come in to him, and will sup with him, and he with me."* The experience of this inward communion, this spiritual participation of the Lord's Supper, is that which we desire to promote among the professors of Christianity; believing with the Apostle; "that the kingdom of God is not meat and drink; but righteousness, and peace, and joy in the Holy Ghost: for he that in these things serveth Christ, is acceptable to God, and approved of men."†

Our dissent from the generality of Christians, on the subjects of Water Baptism and the Supper, and our disuse of these and other ceremonies, have, however, brought upon us much censure from some of our fellow Christians, who have even denied us a right to that name, conceiving that we could not be sincere

* Rev. iii. 20.   † Rom. xiv. 17 and 18.

believers in Christ. But our disuse of these cere-monies, is so far from proceeding from any infe-rior views of Christianity, that it arises from our very high opinion of it; on which ground we cannot reconcile these external rites to the great objects, and particularly to the spirituality of the gospel dispensation. We believe in Christ Jesus, the Saviour of men; we believe that he " washed us from our sins in his own blood;"* that he is " our passover, who is sacri-ficed for us ;"† and that he has " abolished in his flesh, the enmity, even the law of command-ments, contained in ordinances; for through Him we have access, by one Spirit, unto the Father."‡

* Rev. i. 5. † 1 Cor. v. 7.

‡ Ephes. ii. 15 and 18.

CHAPTER VII.

ON THE RELIGIOUS OBSERVANCE OF DAYS AND TIMES.

Exemption from censure claimed for their non-observance. —The observance of them disapproved by the Apostle Paul.—More injurious than beneficial to Religion— especially Festivals.—Setting apart one day in the week approved.—On Public Fasts, &c.—Conclusion from Rom. xiv. 5, &c.

OUR disuse of the religious observance of Days and Times, is generally known, and we trust that, both on this and the preceding subject, we may claim that exemption from censure, which the apostle granted to the church at Colosse: " Let no man judge you in meat or in drink, or in respect of an holy day, or of the new moon, or of the Sabbath days, which are a shadow of things to come; but the body is of Christ."*

By the law of Moses, many days and times were set apart, for the commemoration of various extraordinary circumstances, and for other

* Col. ii. 16. &c.

considerations connected with that dispensation. Some of these were, for a time, observed by the primitive Christians, especially by the Jewish converts, whose attachment to their law, as is already remarked, not only induced them to retain many of its ceremonies, but also to endeavour to impose them on the Gentile Christians. This the apostle Paul was particularly concerned to break through, and to assert the freedom of the gospel dispensation, from the obligation of these legal observances; and though he wished the believers not to judge one another, either for observing, or not observing days and times; yet he could not but consider it an unfavourable symptom in the Galatians, that they should, after having laid them aside, return to the observance of them : " How turn ye again to the weak and beggarly elements, whereunto ye desire again to be in bondage? Ye observe days, and months, and times, and years: I am afraid of you, lest I have bestowed upon you labour in vain."*

Unless those who are in this practice, can prove some command or injunction for it in the New Testament, of which I know not any, I

* Gal. iv. 9, 10, and 11.

-conceive but little more need be said on this subject. If any think the observance tends to promote piety and virtue, we would not judge those who are inclined to make this use of it; but I apprehend it is a fact of too much public notoriety, not to be acknowledged, that observances of this kind, particularly the festivals, are in general so conducted as to promote dissipation and intemperance, much more than piety and virtue; and, therefore, in every point of view, we think we are well warranted in laying such observances aside.

We however consider the setting apart of one day in seven for cessation from business, and for religious services, no more than a reasonable duty: and we encourage the observance of it among our members. It has been our practice from the commencement of our religious society; and although we do not consider the First, or any day of the week, as possessing a superior degree of holiness; yet we believe considerable advantages to religion and virtue arise, not only from a proper dedication and employment of it, but even from the imperfect observance, with which it is on the whole regarded.

We are also sensible that the duties of humiliation and thanksgiving, are frequently incumbent upon us; yet, from the conviction that the qualification to perform these duties, should proceed from a higher source than man, we do not consider it right, to unite with those who set apart particular times, and adopt set forms, for these purposes. Besides this general reason, the occasion is often such as we can, by no means, join with. When war, or the successes or defeats attendant upon it, are the occasion of public-thanksgiving or humiliation, our sentiments on the inconsistency of war with the spirit of Christianity, prevent our uniting in prayer or praises for victories, which involve the destruction of our fellow-creatures: and by which, there is too much reason to fear, many souls are sent unprepared into an awful eternity. By joining on these occasions, we conceive that we should act inconsistently with that peaceable Spirit, which our blessed Lord has so strongly inculcated, and which will be more particularly treated of in the following chapter.

After giving these reasons for our dissent on this subject, I shall conclude with the words of the apostle Paul: " One man esteemeth one

day above another; another esteemeth every day alike. Let every man be fully persuaded in his own mind. He that regardeth the day, regardeth it to the Lord; and he that regardeth not the day to the Lord, he doth not regard it."*
" Let us not therefore judge one another any more : but judge this rather, that no man put a stumbling-block, or an occasion to fall, in his brother's way."†

* Rom. xiv. 5, 6.   † Ibid. 13.

CHAP. VIII.

ON OATHS AND WAR.

Quotations from Matt. v.— *Oaths unnecessary.—Arguments in favour of them answered.—Arguments in favour of War answered.—The Christian Religion the only remedy for this evil.*

" YE have heard, that it hath been said by them of old time, Thou shalt not forswear thyself; but shalt perform unto the Lord thine oaths : but I say unto you, Swear not at all ; neither by heaven, for it is God's throne; nor by the earth, for it is his footstool—But let your communication be yea, yea ; nay, nay ; for whatsoever is more than these cometh of evil."

" Ye have heard that it hath been said, An eye for an eye, and a tooth for a tooth : but I say unto you, that ye resist not evil.—Ye have heard that it hath been said, Thou shalt love thy neighbour and hate thine enemy : but I say unto you, Love your enemies ; bless them that curse you ; do good to them that hate you ; and pray for them which despitefully use you and

g 2

persecute you; that ye may be the children of
your Father which is in heaven; for he maketh
his sun to rise on the evil and on the good; and
sendeth rain on the just and on the unjust."*

After reciting these strong and unequivocal
injunctions of our Divine Master, I have paused
to consider, whether I should say a word more
on the subject of them; their own force and
perspecuity seeming to require no comment. I
shall therefore make none upon them; but after
saying that on these, and other similar passages
in the Scriptures, we ground our testimony
against oaths and war, shall proceed to consider
the objections that are made, to the adoption of
precepts so clearly conveyed to us, and the
practice of which would be attended with so
many benefits to mankind.

With respect to oaths, the apparent necessity
of them is so small, and their real injury is so
great, by profaning the sacred name, that, it is
presumed, very few religiously minded people,
will be disposed to plead in their favour: and,
indeed, it appears to me difficult to find an
objection of any importance, to laying them
wholly aside.

* Matt. v. 33, 34, 35, 36, 37, 38, 39, 43, 44, 45.

The principnl arguments used by those who are disposed to plead for them, must however be considered. One of these is, that the Almighty is sometimes said, in scripture, to make use of an oath. To this it may be answered, that the Almighty could not swear as man swears, there being none greater than Himself to whom he could appeal ; or to whom He was amenable for the truth of his declaration. Besides which, we apprehend, that what He might do, as Sovereign Lord, may not be proper for us to do as dependant creatures, whose highest perfection is obedience to His will; and this will being expressly revealed to us in this instance by his beloved Son, our obvious duty is to comply with it.

Another argument in favour of swearing before magistrates, is advanced from the circumstance of our Lord's being silent before the High Priest, until he adjured him by the living God. That the High Priest intended formally to administer a judicial oath to our Saviour, is what, I apprehend, the context will not support. It rather appears, that Caiaphas, being irritated by our Lord's silence, made use of this expression in the violence of his temper, and not in a judicial capacity; and until the latter can be proved, our Lord's simple reply : "Thou hast said,"* in no degree partakes of the nature of an oath.

A third argument in favour of the use of oaths, is drawn from some expressions of the apostle Paul; as, "God is my witness;"† "I charge thee before God,"‡ &c. These, and other similar expressions, do not, however, appear to constitute an oath ; nor would they be admitted as such in a court of judicature. In the beginning of our society, such expressions were sometimes offered to magistrates, instead of an oath, but always refused.§   Besides, if these words of the Apostle are to be considered as oaths, they would prove too much, by showing that he used them in private correspondence, or communication ; which those who plead for judicial swearing, agree our Lord meant to prohibit, by the command, " Swear not at all."

* Matt. xxvi. 64.   † Rom. i. 9.   ‡ 2 Tim. iv. 1.

§ The first affirmation granted to our society instead of an oath, was a declaration " In the presence of Almighty God." But this not affording universal relief, the legislature afterwards indulged us with the present form of attestation, in which there is no use of the sacred Name.

Some have also argued in favour of judicial swearing, from an allusion to it in the epistle to the Hebrews, chap. vi. 16. But surely the incidental mention of a general practice among "men," is not a sufficient argument for the rectitude of that practice; nor a proof that it was allowed by Christians, who, in comparison with the rest of mankind, were then few in number.

It may, perhaps, be still argued, that the ends of justice could not be answered without an oath. To this it may be replied, that if the same penalty were annexed to a false affirmation, as to a false oath, those whose consciences are not sufficiently tender to preserve them from giving a false affirmation, would find, in the penalty, as much terror from offending against one, as against the other.

It has been alleged by some, that this prohibition of oaths relates only to common conversation; but the context will by no means support this construction, as will appear from the following considerations. First, Profane swearing was prohibited under the law, and it is evident that Christ was forbidding what the law had allowed. Secondly, Swearing is here contrasted with forswearing or false swearing. Now this being contrary to the law, whether before a magistrate, or in private conversation, the command not to swear at all must be equally extensive. Our construction of the command of Christ, is further confirmed by the exhortation of his disciple and apostle, James: "Above all things, my brethren, swear not; neither by heaven, neither by earth, neither by *any other oath*: but let your yea, be yea, and your nay, nay, lest you fall into condemnation."*

Having said what appears to be sufficient on the subject of oaths; we come next to consider the arguments used in defence of war. Of these the principal one is, that it is unavoidable and necessary. In reply to this we say, that so long as mankind are disposed to live under the influence of their passions, and to sacrifice their dearest interests to their avarice, or their ambition, this plea will not be wanting. But let us consider what proofs have been given, that war is really unavoidable. Has any nation fairly made the experiment, and failed? Where is the country that has regulated its conduct by that justice,

* James v. 12.

that liberality, that love, that humility, and that meekness, which Christianity requires, and yet has found war unavoidable? Can we contemplate the characters of the individuals, who have been the rulers of nations, and say, that such have been the dispositions which regulated their public and private conduct; and that still they have not been able to preserve their country from war and bloodshed? Till all this can be clearly proved, the argument from necessity is of no weight.

If, then, it cannot be shown that men, living and acting in a truly Christian spirit, have found war to be necessary and unavoidable, the argument assumed must be considered as destitute of foundation. But, that I may not be thought to reason chimerically, I shall show that a people have existed, who, acting upon these Christian principles, preserved their country from war and bloodshed; even while their neighbours were frequently involved in them. Pennsylvania, it is generally known, was originally the property of one called a Quaker, who filled most of the offices of the government, with persons of his own persuasion. Had not the conduct of this people towards their neighbours, both Indians

5

and Europeans, been recorded by men totally
unconnected with the society, my relation might
appear partial and interested ; but history, impartial history, has transmitted the conduct of
this people to posterity, in such a manner, as
renders it unnecessary for me to say more, than
that, so long as they retained their ascendancy
in the state, which was about sixty or seventy
years, neither internal nor external war, was
permitted to disturb their peaceful habitations.*
We do not say that occasions of difference
never occurred : but other means of settling
their differences, than those generally resorted
to, were pursued; and, if not found successful,
submission was wisely preferred to the precarious and violent decision of the sword.

* In corroboration of these circumstances, the following quota-
tion is given from the translation of a Latin Poem, entituled
"Descriptio Pennsylvaniæ," and written in 1729, by Thomas
Makin, after forty years residence in Pennsylvania :

"On just and fairest terms the land is gained,
No force of arms has any right obtained.
'Tis here, without the use of arms, alone,
The blest inhabitant enjoys his own.
Here many, to their wish, in peace enjoy
Their happy Lots, and nothing doth annoy.
But sad New England's different conduct shows
What dire effect from injured Indians flows."

See Proud's History of Pennsylvania, p. 211—Note.

Great pains are taken to make a distinction between offensive and defensive war; and whilst the former is generally reprobated, the latter meets with many advocates. It must, I suppose, be admitted, that in almost every war, both parties profess to act on the principle of defense: and where is the criterion which accurately determines the difference? But supposing an extreme case, and that without any provocation, one man, or one nation, is attacked by another, is there no dependance to be placed on a superintending Providence? and have religion and virtue no resources, but in the arm of flesh? Were our minds brought into a true Christian state, the protection of Divine Providence would be humbly and safely relied upon; so far, at least, as to prevent us from seeking redress, by means destructive of the lives of our fellow-creatures.

Such is the natural state of mankind, that "offences must needs come;" but it ought to be remembered, "that wo is to him, by whom the offence cometh." Were those dispositions recommended by our blessed Lord, cherished by that which considers itself the offended party, it would soon appear, that war is not so necessary and unavoidable, as is by many imagined.

If sound policy were adopted, it would unite with true Christianity, in eradicating this distressing evil. Can any thing in this world compensate for the desolation and misery, which war occasions in the earth? To the loss of life and property, with almost all worldly comforts, let us add the still more important loss, which religion and virtue sustain from a state of war, and from the military life in general: Will it not then be difficult to conceive how men, who really have, what they think, the good of their country at heart, and who also consider themselves entitled to the denomination of Christians, can promote a practice, which is productive of so many, both natural and moral evils? In contemplating this distressing subject, we find it necessary to have recourse to that Christian charity, which it is our duty to extend to those, who differ from us in principle and practice."* I wish, how-

* Our excellent apologist, R. Barclay, manifests the liberality of his mind on this subject, when, after arguing, with his usual ability, in favour of our principle against war, he admits that the practice of non-resistance is the most perfect part of the Christian religion, and makes considerable allowances for those who differ from us on this occasion.—See Prop. xv. close of Sect. 15.

ever, for myself and my fellow professors, that
we may faithfully maintain our principles on
this subject; being at the same time careful to
support the doctrine of peace, in the spirit of
peace: then we may be made instrumental, in
promoting the increase of the government of
the son of God, whose introduction into this
world was announced by an angel, occompanied
with "a multitude of the heavenly host; prais-
ing God, and saying: Glory to God in the
highest, and on earth Peace, Good-will towards
men."*

There are a few arguments brought forward
in favour of war, from some passages in the New
Testament, which it will be proper to consider.
Of these, the principal one is, the expression of
our Lord to his disciples : " He that hath no
sword, let him sell his garment and buy one."†
This passage is generally considered to be of
doubtful signification ; and some, who do not
agree with us in our sentiments on war, consider
this expression of our Lord as allegorical.‡
When the disciples replied: "Here are two

---

* Luke ii. 13 and 14.　　　† See Luke xxii 36.

‡ See Dr. Edwards on the Style, &c. of the Scripture,
page 126.

swords," he gave this short answer: " It is enough."* This seems to imply that they did not understand his meaning; for if he had intended the external sword, how could two be sufficient for the number of the disciples, and at a time when they were about to be attacked by a multitude, that came out, as against a thief, with swords and staves? But what seems clearly to show, that our Saviour did not intend to recommend the use of the sword in a literal sense, is the circumstance which occurred very soon after he had used the expression under consideration : for we find, that when Peter, on the very same day, made use of a sword in defence of his master, he was reproved by him in this manner : " Put up again thy sword into his place; for all they that take the sword, shall perish with the sword."† It may also be added, that it was on the same, or the succeeding day, that our Lord said to Pilate : " My kingdom is not of this world. If my kingdom were of this world, then would my servants fight, that I should not be delivered to the Jews."‡ Now, when these important and concurring circumstances are considered, can it be supposed, that our Lord intended to recommend to his disciples

* Luke xxii. 38.   † Mat. xxvi. 52.   ‡ John xviii. 36.

the use of the sword, either in defence of Him or themselves, or on any other occasion ?

Another circumstance brought forward as an argument in favour of war, is the conversion of Cornelius, a centurion in the Roman army, and no account given of his having relinquished a military life.* As we have not any further ac-count of this pious centurion, than that of his conversion, and the circumstances attending it, no argument of any weight can be drawn from this relation. Some ancient writers inform us, that the primitive Christians did not fight; and we may therefore reasonably suppose, that if the centurion continued firm in his attachment to the Christian religion, he abandoned his military life. At any rate, the silence of the sacred historian cannot, with propriety, be brought forward as an argument in support of war; or as showing it to be consistent with the Christian dispensation.

It is further argued, that the expression of the apostle Paul, who says respecting the ma-

* Acts x. The remarks on this case apply to that of the centurion mentioned Mat. viii, 5.

gistrate : " He beareth not the sword in vain,"*
is an implied acknowledgment of the propriety
of using the sword in a military manner.   This
argument, I conceive, arises from a misapplication of the passage.   The sword here alluded
to, we have reason to suppose, was only an
emblem of civil power.   We are informed, that
one of the chief magistrates in Rome, and it
is to the Romans the Apostle uses this expression, had a sword hung up in his court, as an
emblem of his power;† and we know that in
this country, especially in corporate towns, the
chief magistrates have a sword borne before
them on particular occasions, as an emblem of
office.   But if the sword was even used in the
punishment of offenders, it would be no fair
argument in favour of using it, for the purposes
of war, and those devastations attendant on this
lamentable evil.

These, and such as these, are the arguments
advanced by many, in support of an evil, which,
in its consequences, shocks humanity, destroys
morality, weakens the influence of religion, and
entails on mankind miseries incalculable and

* Rom. xiii. 4.
† Godwin's Roman Antiquities, p. 164.

indescribable. Was the ingenuity of man as much exercised to put an end to this calamity, as his ambition is to support it, we should soon find the benefits resulting from this disposition. But it is religion, it is the Christian religion, which alone provides an adequate remedy for this malignant disorder; and when mankind are willing to receive it, in the purity, the love, the meekness, and the humility, which its Divine Author inculcated, this, with other similar predictions respecting him, will be fulfilled: " He shall judge among the nations, and work conviction* among many peoples; and they shall beat their swords into plough-shares, and their spears into pruning-hooks: nation shall not lift up sword against nation; neither shall they learn war any more."†

* See Lowth's Translation of Isaiah.

† Isaiah ii. 4.

CHAP. IX.

ON AMUSEMENTS.

General remarks on them.—Rules respecting them.—On Dancing and Music.—Necessity of properly regulating amusements for youth.—Propriety of avoiding temptation.

THE little benefit, and great injury, which attend most of those enjoyments, that go under the name of amusements, have induced us to bring them into less compass, than the generality of Christians do : not that we are averse to such relaxations from bodily or mental exercise, as become rational beings, and true Christians : but the repugnancy of a great part of those pleasures to religion and virtue, and the avidity with which they are pursued, are causes of sorrow to those, who have at heart the real interests, temporal and spiritual, of their fellow-creatures.

There are three rules relating to amusements, by which our conduct should be regulated.

1.—To avoid all those which tend needlessly to oppress and injure any part of the animal creation. Of this class are cock-fighting and horse-racing : also hunting, &c. when engaged in for diversion and pleasure.

2.—To abstain from such as are connected with a spirit of hazardous enterprise; by which the property and temporal happiness of individuals and families, are often made to depend on the most precarious circumstances; and the gain of one, frequently entails misery on many. Of this class are all games in which property is staked.

3.—To avoid such as expose us to unnecessary temptations, with respect to our virtue; or, which dissipate the mind, so as to render a return to civil and religious duties ungrateful. Of this kind, stage entertainments are peculiarly to be avoided, with various other places of public amusement, which have a tendency to corrupt the heart, or to alienate it from the love and fear of God.

The amusements of dancing and music, we think, also come within this class. It may be alleged, that these might be practised in such a manner, as not to accord with the description given. Our Society, however, thinks it right to abstain from those amusements ; both because of their frequent connection with places and circumstances, which are highly objectionable; and because we conceive they can scarcely be entered into, without an improper employment of that time, which we are required not to waste, but to pass in fear, and to redeem.

Were our minds rightly regulated, and our affections set on things above, very little, which is called amusement, would be thought necessary for those who are arrived at mature age. With respect to young people, it peculiarly behooves those who have the care of them, to see that such amusements only be adopted, as may not prove injurious to their religion or virtue ; but which may tend to promote their possessing a sound mind in a sound body. Were amusements thus restrained and regulated, great would be the benefit arising from such restrictions ; but when we see how ardently many, not only of the youth, but even of those who are considerably advanced in years, rush into dissipating and corrupting pleasures, it is not to be wondered at, that vice and irreligion should prevail to an alarming degree.

We ought ever to retain a sense of our own weakness, and of our aptitude to fall into temptations, when they are presented to us. Were we properly concerned for our own most important interest, that of our immortal souls, this sense would lead us to avoid, and not to run into, temptation. How much those amusements are either evils themselves, or temptations to evil, it cannot be necessary to point out at large, to those who exercise serious reflection. How necessary is it, therefore, to attend to the apostolic exhortation : " See then that ye walk circumspectly, not as fools, but as wise, redeeming the time, because the days are evil!"*

* Ephes. v. 15, 16.

CHAP. X.

ON DRESS AND ADDRESS.

Our principle for regulating dress.—Scripture passages in support of it.—An objection answered.—Nonconformity to the world to be accompanied with the transformation of the mind. Our peculiarities of address supported by reason, by propriety, and by religion.—On not taking off the hat.—Custom too much admitted in the conduct of Christians.

ON the first of these subjects, our principle is, to let decency, utility, and simplicity, be our chief guides; and not to conform to the change-able fashions, of a vain and fluctuating world; though we may occasionally adopt alterations, which are convenient or useful. This is a principle, the propriety of which, I apprehend, no one will deny; and it is easy to suppose, that such a rule must make those who adopt it, generally singular in their appearance. It is not, however, for the sake of singularity, that we appear different from others; yet we have reason to believe, that even this singularity is not without its use. It is, in some respects, like a hedge about us; which, though it does not make the ground it encloses rich and fruitful, yet frequently prevents those intrusions, by which the labour of the husbandman is injured or destroyed.

The conduct which we have adopted in this respect, is supported by many passages in holy writ. " Be not conformed to this world; but be ye transformed by the renewing of your mind,"* was the advice of the apostle to the Christians, who dwelt at the seat of Roman grandeur and luxury; and at a time, when this grandeur and luxury had perhaps attained to their greatest height. As the female sex has generally been accounted most prone to excesses of this kind, the apostles, in writing on this subject, have more particularly addressed their advices to them: thus Paul says: " I will that women adorn themselves with modest apparel; with shamefacedness and sobriety; not with broidered hair, or gold, or pearls, or costly array, but, which becometh women professing godliness, with good works."† The following is extracted from the apostle Peter's advice to Christian wives: " Whose adorning let it not

* Rom. xii. 2.   † 1 Tim. ii. 9, 10.

be that outward adorning of plaiting the hair,
or of wearing of gold, or of putting on of apparel; but let it be the hidden man of the heart
in that which is not corruptible; even the orna-
ment of a meek and quiet spirit, which is in the
sight of God of great price."*

It has been objected to us, that we connect
religion too much with dress. This, I conceive,
arises from a misapprehension of our principles.
We consider simplicity of apparel and a nonconformity to vain fashions, as a moral virtue,
in the same manner, though not to the same degree, as we do temperance and sobriety. In these
it is possible a man may be very exemplary,
and yet be a stranger to true religion : but because this man wants that which should be the
moving spring, of all our good actions, and,
perhaps, in some other parts of conduct, is even
deficient in morality, no one, surely, would recommend such a man to lay aside that part of
moral conduct, which he is already in the practice of. Thus it is with our apparel. We
need not lay aside what is right in one part of
our practice, because we are not thought right,
or do not think ourselves so, in every thing.

* 1 Pet. iii. 3, 4.

A man's pretension to religion or virtue, should not be estimated from the plainness of his dress and outward appearance, any more than from his possessing some other moral virtues, into which true religion would, no doubt, lead him.

It is however highly important to us, to maintain something more than the form of godliness; and, whilst we avoid a conformity to this world, to be careful to seek after that Divine Power, which will enable us to comply with the other part of the exhortation: " Be ye transformed by the renewing of your mind, that ye may prove what is that good, and acceptable, and perfect will of God."* Thus, having our minds and conduct rightly regulated, we shall fulfil another important, apostolic injunction : " Let not then your good be evil spoken of."†

In our address also, there are some peculiarities, which it will be proper to explain; as our using the singular number, in speaking to a single person ; our disuse of the appellations of master, mistress, &c. in a complimentary man-

* Rom. xii. 2.   † Ibid. xiv. 16.

H

ner, to those who do not stand in these relations to us; and our calling the months and
days of the week by their numerical names, instead of those which are derived from the heathen deities, &c.   From these, and other erroneous and corrupt practices, the Spirit of Truth,
in which we profess to believe, as guiding
into all truth, led our predecessors in religious profession; and, we believe, still leads
us, as we faithfully follow it.   Our conduct in
these respects is so well supported by the
practices mentioned in holy writ, as well as by
the simplicity and reasonableness of it, that I
apprehend no one will deny its propriety, even
if they will not allow it to be necessary.

The origin of applying the plural number to
an individual, and of giving complimentary
titles to one another, will, I suppose, be acknowledged, by those who have traced these
things to their source, to have been vanity or
pride.   Besides this consideration, our practice
of using the singular number to a single person,
and of calling one another by the proper name,
is both more correct and more perspicuous.
This is also the case with respect to our names
of days and months.   Nevertheless, it is not by

reason and propriety alone, that our conduct in these things may be supported ; nor are these the grounds of our peculiar practice. Religion, if an attention to the examples and precepts recorded in the Holy Scriptures, has a claim to the name of religion, also justifies our conduct. It was, no doubt, in allusion to the complimentary, and not to the proper, use of the appellations of Rabbi, Father, and Master, that our Lord prohibited the practice among his followers. Speaking of the disposition of the Scribes and Pharisees, he says : " They love the uppermost rooms at feasts, and the chief seats in the synagogues, and greetings in the markets, and to be called of men, Rabbi, Rabbi."* Then, addressing himself to the multitude and to his disciples, he adds: " But be not ye called Rabbi : for one is your master, even Christ ; and all ye are brethren. And call no man your father upon earth ; for one is your Father, which is in heaven. Neither be ye called masters : for one is your master, even Christ."† The following expressions of Elihu, a pious young man, mentioned in the book of Job, are also applicable to our present purpose : " Let me not, I pray you, accept any man's person ;

* Matt. xxiii. 6, 7.   † Ib. 8, 9, 10.

neither let me give flattering titles unto man; for I know not to give flattering titles: in so doing, my Maker would soon take me away."*

With respect to the use of the singular number to a single person, it is the uniform practice in the Holy Scriptures; and indeed in all other writings, to a period of time long posterior to that in which the last part of the Scriptures was written. It is not, therefore, to be expected, that any allusion to a contrary practice should be mentioned in them. We think, however, that we may consider our conduct, in this respect, consistent with that " form of sound words,"† recommended by Paul to Timothy.

The giving of the names of heathen deities, &c. to days and months, is not only inconsistent with " the form of sound words" just mentioned; but also contrary to the spirit of the injunction given to the Israelites, as a preservative from contaminating themselves with idolatry: "In all things that I have said unto you, be circumspect: and make no mention of the name of other gods; neither let it be heard out of thy

* Job xxxii. 21, 22.   † 2 Tim. i. 13.

mouth."*ₐ It may also be remembered, that when the reformation of the Jews was foretold by the prophets, these, amongst other things, were stated as a part: "I will take the name of Baalim out of her mouth,"† "I will turn to the people a pure language;"‡ and "I will cut off the names of the idols out of the land, and they shall no more be remembered."§

There is another peculiarity in our conduct, on which it may be proper to say a few words. Our refusal to take off the hat, as a mark of respect to man, is generally known. The reason for this is, that it is a token of reverence enjoined and used, in our solemn approaches to the Supreme Being; when exercising the religious duties of preaching or prayer. On this account, and not from any disrespect to our

* Exodus xxiii. 13.

a See also Deut. xii. 2.   Joshua xxiii. 7.   Ps. xvi. 4.

† Hosea ii. 17.   ‡ Zephaniah iii. 9.

§ Zechariah xiii. 2.   The following lines are not inapplicable to this subject :—

"The Pagan page how far more wise than ours !
They with the gods they worshipped graced their song:
Our song we grace with gods we disbelieve ;
Retain the manners, but reject the creed."

HANNAH MORE.

H 3

superiors, we think it right not to confound
this solemn act of reverence to the Almighty,
with the marks of respect to our fellow creatures.   True civility and due respect may be
better shown by conduct, than by compliment:
and we are far from desiring to dismiss those
social duties from our attention and regard.

Many are apt to plead general custom, as a
sanction to practices, which, were they impartially examined, would be acknowledged to be
erroneous and improper : and it is to be regretted, that the professors of Christianity, should
retain so much that is inconsistent with its
purity and simplicity.   If these things cannot
be styled " the weightier matters of the law,"*
and we allow they cannot, yet, we believe, they
may be considered, as the externals of religion,
and as things which we " ought not to leave
undone."

* Matt. xxiii. 23.

CHAP. XI.

ON CIVIL GOVERNMENT.

Peaceableness of our principles a security to Government.— *Duties of subjects.* — *Suffering peaceably submitted to, when active compliance cannot be conscientiously rendered. —Civil and religious liberty valued, and how best defended.*

THE peaceableness of our principles, when applied even to enemies, affords a strong security to any government under which we live, that we cannot unite in any practices, with a view either to injure or subvert it. The consideration of this circumstance, attended with a correspondent conduct, has probably been the means of obtaining indulgencies for some of our principles, which are contrary to general laws. Several of these principles, are such as generally to exclude us from becoming a constituent part of government: what we have, therefore, to consider are the duties of subjects.

These duties are clearly defined in the New Testament; and under circumstances which render this definition peculiarly strong. When they were enjoined, the primitive Christians were frequently under persecution; the government, at that time, was of a kind which is generally considered the worst, and in the hands of the worst of men; nevertheless, we see no encouragement given to any thing like sedition or resistance. On the contrary, the believers in Christ were taught to "be subject unto the higher powers,"* "to obey magistrates,"† and to "submit to every ordinance of man for the Lord's sake.—As free and not using liberty for a cloak of maliciousness, but as the servants of God."‡ These are the principles on which our Society, as a body, have uniformly acted, as may be seen by the advices given on this subject, in a Book of Extracts from advices of the Yearly Meeting, printed in London, in the year 1802. From page 19 of this book, the following advice is taken: "We trust we are called to show forth to the world, in life and practice, that the blessed reign of the Messiah, the Prince of Peace, is begun; and we doubt not but it will proceed, till it attain its completion in the earth: when, according to the prophecies of Isaiah and Micah, "nation shall not lift up sword against nation; neither shall they learn war any more." Influenced by these principles, we cannot consistently join with such, as form

---

* Rom. xiii. 1.   † Titus iii. 1.   ‡ 1 Pet. ii. 13, 16.

combinations of a hostile nature against any; much less in opposition to those placed in sovereign or subordinate authority; nor can we unite with, or encourage, such as revile and asperse them; for it is written: "Thou shalt not speak evil of the ruler of thy people."—Yearly Meeting's printed epistle, 1775.

But whilst we think it right to put in practice the advices given to the primitive Christians on this subject, we are, as they were, under circumstances, which sometimes prevent us from actively complying, with what the laws of the country require. Nevertheless, we submit to the law, by suffering the peaceable execution of it, in cases in which we cannot actively comply. There are duties which we owe to our consciences and to God, with which human power cannot dispense, and of which it is not a competent judge. The government of conscience is God's prerogative; and when it is neither used as a cloak of maliciousness, nor abused to the disturbance of the public peace, it ought to be fully free. Our Society in this country, though under some circumstances which bear rather hard upon it, has abundant cause for gratitude to the government, for the favors we enjoy; and it is to be hoped, that we shall always conduct ourselves so as to merit the continuance, and even the extension of them; "being obliged to demean ourselves, not only as a grateful people, but, as a Christian society, to live peaceably and inoffensively, under the present government, as we have always done, under the various revolutions of government, ever since we were a people."—Yearly Meeting's written epistle, 1692.

But, notwithstanding our peaceable and submissive principles, in relation to those who are placed in authority over us, we are far from being insensible to the value of civil and religious liberty. When these are violated, we think it right to represent our grievances to those who oppress us, or who have it in their power to afford relief. If this be done in a Christian spirit, and in a language respectfully strong, it would be found, in general, a much more successful, and always a more proper, means of obtaining redress, than any seditious and turbulent proceedings, or those bloody appeals to the sword, to which mankind are too apt to resort, as the relief of oppression, or the gratification of revenge.

CHAP. XII.

ON DISCIPLINE.

The necessity of discipline in religious societies.—Objections
to it answered. — Particular objects of our discipline
enumerated.—Different meetings in which it is trans-
acted.—Importance of transacting it in a right spirit.

WHATEVER may be the inducement of
any people to form themselves into a separate
society, it must be on some principles which
they assume, and on the preservation of which
their continuance, as a particular society, must,
in a great measure, depend. It is also the duty
of every society, formed upon religious principles, to support good morals, without which its
pretensions to religion are vain. These two
considerations render discipline, in a religious
society, necessary to its reputable existence;
and when they are not attended to, confusion
and disgrace must follow. However excellent
any of our religious principles may be, we who
profess them are all frail and fallible. We are
all by nature prone to evil: and if we have

even experienced some degree of redemption
from the state of fallen nature, we are still
liable, without watchfulness, to fall, or to
be drawn aside in principle or practice.
Hence we find, in all religious societies,
those who are a discredit to their profession; and we are far from considering ourselves free from such disreputable members.
But, in order to remedy this evil, as much as
possible, we have a discipline established among
us, the first object of which is, to labour in
gospel love, and by private advice, for the reformation of those who walk disorderly; and if
this cannot be effected, and the nature of the
case require it, to disown such persons as members of our society. The reasonableness of this
discipline appears so evident, that it may seem
unnecessary to enter into further arguments in
favour of its propriety and utility; yet, as objections are advanced against our practice in
this respect, it may be proper to take some
notice of them.

The objections commonly advanced against
the exercise of discipline are, *first*, that it lays
an unnecessary restraint on private judgment;
secondly, that it interferes with that attention to

the dictates of the Spirit, to which we are indivi-
dually recommended ; and *thirdly*, that the dis-
owning of members is a species of persecution.

The necessity of discipline, for the constitu-
tion and support of any religious society, has
already been stated, so as, in a great measure, to
obviate the first objection. It may, however,
be proper to add, that in every society, civil or
religious, submission to the regulations of that
society is necessary, in order to prevent the
licentiousness and confusion, which would follow, if every member acted upon his own ideas,
without any external restriction. If this be applicable to society in general, it is particularly
so, with regard to those religious societies,
which have separated from all others, on account of opinions and practices, that appear to
them not consistent with the nature of true religion, or unnecessarily attached to it. How
shall a society retain its existence with any degree of propriety, if those who depart from, or
disavow its principles, are to remain members
of it ? And how shall such a society be known
to the world, if its members are permitted to profess and act differently, even on subjects which
at first formed the foundation of their union?

It has been said, that nothing except immorality and the fundamentals of religion, should be the subjects of discipline. But, if we could be all of one mind, on the application of the word immorality, we should find it very difficult to agree on the fundamentals of religion; and the number of persons is, perhaps, not small, who would resolve these fundamentals into a belief of a God, and of the immortality of the soul. We may easily consider, what a strange medley, the liberty contended for, would admit into one society. The Jew, the Christian, the Mahomedan, and the Heathen, with their various subdivisions, might all be blended together in one body; in which we may suppose, if any right zeal for their respective religious sentiments should exist, there would be perpetual jarring and discord. Much more conducive is it to the peace of religious societies, that each should consistently maintain its own principles, and either suffer those who dissent from them, quietly to withdraw; or, after proper labour and waiting for restoration, to disown them as acknowledged members of the society. When this is done, as it ought to be, in a right spirit, it is no violation of true charity, nor of that liberty which all have, no doubt, a right to exercise with respect to private opinion.

The second objection is often urged in a
manner, which may tend to mislead, and capti-
vate the unwary; but it proceeds on a supposition, which is by no means admissible, namely,
that a body of Christians, united in the belief
of certain principles, is more likely to be misled,
than some of the individuals constituting that
body. It has always been the judgment of our
Society, that the establishment of meetings for
discipline, was under the same Divine influence,
which originally formed our predecessors a
distinct people. The subjects of the care of
these meetings have varied very little from their
first institution; and, therefore, for any persons
now to pretend, that this discipline is an improper restraint on the leadings of the Spirit,
so far as respects them, is to say, in effect, that
they are not led by the same Spirit in which the
Society professes to believe, and by which it
desires ever to be led. " The spirits of the
prophets are subject to the prophets;"* and
the individuals of a religious society must be
subject to that society collectively; otherwise
anarchy and confusion will ensue : and when it
is considered, that in our society, a much greater
proportion of its members concur in forming

* 1 Cor. xiv. 32.

its rules, than in any other, there seems no room left for objections like this. They might have a more specious appearance, if the power of making rules and regulations were lodged in a few individuals : though even in this case, they would be destitute of solidity, if the individuals were properly delegated.

The comparison between persecution and the disownment of the members of a religious society, has been often zealously urged, by some of the advocates for unrestrained liberty of sentiment. To draw this comparison the stronger with respect to our society, it has been urged, that they who are deprived of membership with us, lose not only the common privileges of membership, but, if reduced to poverty, are deprived of that provision, for the support and education of the poor, for which the society is peculiarly distinguished. But this argument, by proving too much, proves nothing : for even these latitudinarians would, I suppose, think it right to disown a member for idolatry or atheism ; and yet, on such a one, it would not be proper to inflict what may be termed persecution. But, are we, because we make extraordinary provision for our poor, to retain all that have been members, however they may differ from us in principle or practice? The absurdity of the argument, appears to me too great to need further confutation. What is sometimes advanced, with respect to degradation of character by disownment, it is apprehended, stands or falls with the former. If the society has, by its general good conduct, obtained such a degree of reputation, that those who are disowned by it, lose part of the good opinion of the public; must it sacrifice that reputation, by retaining in its bosom, those who violate its rules, or trample upon its principles: principles, for the support of which, our predecessors in religious profession, were willing to suffer much ignominy; with the loss of property, of liberty, and even of life itself?

Besides a general oversight of the conduct and conversation of our members, there are other objects which obtain attention in our meetings for discipline. One of the most material of these is, the support of the poor: for it has been the practice in our society, from its first establishment, to maintain our own poor, and not give them occasion to apply for the common modes of relief. Notwithstanding this, we think it right to contribute to the support of the poor who are not of our society, in common with our neighbours; and that, not only in cases where the laws oblige us; but also, when ability is afforded, in those voluntary charities which are established, or occasionally promoted, for the benefit of this part of the community : a class, to the suitable relief and employment of which, much importance is very properly attached.

Another material object in our meetings for discipline, is, due attention to proceedings in relation to marriage; to take care that the parties are clear of other engagements of the same kind; that they are not within disallowed degrees of consanguinity ; and that, in case of previous marriage, the rights of former children be properly secured : after which, care is also exercised, that the marriage be concluded in a proper and becoming manner.

The register of these marriages ; of births and burials ; the care of our meeting-houses and burial-grounds; the admission of members; the granting and receiving of certificates for those who remove from one district to another; the sufferings of our members on account of ecclesiastical and military demands,* with divers other matters ; are also subjects of our care in these meetings.

The meetings in which these matters are transacted, are called Monthly Meetings, from their being held once in every month. They send representatives, and answer queries relative to the general conduct of their members, to other meetings, which are called Quarterly Meetings ; the principal business of which is to superintend Monthly Meetings, and to advise and assist them when occasion may require. These Quarterly Meetings also send representatives, and answer queries to a meeting which is called, the Yearly Meeting. This Meeting has a general oversight of the society ;- and makes rules for its government and welfare.

This description of our meetings for discipline is intended to apply only to the men's meetings : the women also have their Monthly, Quarterly, and Yearly Meetings, in which they attend to the wants of their own sex, and exer-

* It may be proper here to remove a prevailing impression, that the amount of these sufferings is reimbursed to the sufferers. We not only have no funds for this purpose ; but such a practice does not, nor ever did, exist in our Society.

cise a care over their conduct; but have no
power of dismemberment.

The importance of transacting this discipline
in a right spirit, and by those who may be properly qualified, has ever been felt as of no small
importance to its right preservation; and many
are the advices, which have been issued by the
Yearly Meeting on this subject. The following,
being short and comprehensive, will, I apprehend, afford an instructive description of our
concern in this respect: "We tenderly exhort,
that in all your meetings for the discipline of the
church, you wait in humility, to have your
spirits brought into subjection to the Spirit of
Christ; that thereby you may be duly qualified
for the work and service, conducive to the build-
ing up of his church; in which work, all who
are engaged should be men of upright hearts
and clean hands; rightly prepared for the service
they undertake." 1743.

CHAP. XIII.

CONCLUSION.

*Address to the Youth, on the Remembrance of their Creator.
—Reason and Revelation.—The Holy Scriptures and
Christianity.—On our peculiar principles.—On the necessity of regeneration.—Address to persons not of our
religious persuasion.*

IN the design and execution of this work,
my mind has been much influenced, by a desire
for the welfare of the youth in our society,
and for their instruction in the principles of
true religion. To them I feel disposed to address myself in this conclusion.

Let me remind you, my dear friends, of that
wise and pious injunction, "Remember thy
Creator in the days of thy youth."* Consider
his operations in nature and in grace; in Providence and in Redemption. Although in the consideration of all these, some difficulties, not
easily comprehended, may present themselves;
yet so much will be opened to the humble and
attentive mind, as will excite the love and fear

* Eccles. xii. 1.

of Him, "who made the heaven and the earth, the sea, and all that therein is."* In entering into these considerations, there are two assistants afforded us, by our gracious Creator—Reason and Revelation. The former, as well as the latter, is useful on this occasion. It is a faculty given us by God; and, if rightly exercised, will tend to promote our knowledge of Him, particularly in the works of creation and nature. When not misled by the vanity of the human heart, reason sees and feels its own imperfection; and readily embraces and submits to those advantages, which revelation affords. By revelation, I mean to comprehend both that which is mediate, and that which is immediate. The former is communicated in the Holy Scriptures, in which we have very ample accounts of the being and nature of God; of his manifold works in creation and in providence; of his love to mankind, particularly in the work of redemption by Christ; and in affording the assistance of the Holy Spirit, to guide and direct into all necessary truth. It is by this Spirit, which is called the Spirit of God, and of Christ, as proceeding from the Father and the Son, that immediate revelation is received. This revelation pro-

* Psalm cxlvi. 6.

duces that knowledge of God and of Christ, on which eternal life depends. In this sense, "no man knoweth who the Father is, but the Son; and he to whom the Son will reveal him."*
And when it pleases God to reveal his Son in any, and obedience is yielded to the heavenly vision, these then become acquainted with the mysteries of God's kingdom; and are made sensible, that "flesh and blood hath not revealed these things unto them; but their Father which is in Heaven."†

As the holy Scriptures are the blessed means of introducing us to an acquaintance with the way of life and salvation, and of affording us much instruction in our various duties to God, and one to another; I earnestly press on you, my dear young friends, a frequent and serious perusal of them. You will here find much profitable instruction of various kinds : the history is, beyond any other, important and interesting; the mystery makes "wise unto salvation."‡ Here you may see the various dealings of God with his creature man; you may be made acquainted with the dispensation of the law, the predictions of the prophets, the ministration of John, and the most glorious dispen-

* Luke x. 22.   † Matt. xvi. 17.   ‡ 2 Tim. iii. 15.

sation of the gospel. Beware of such publications as have a tendency to create a disrelish for these sacred writings. Consider what the state of our religious knowledge would have been without them; and look at those parts of the world which have not had the benefit of the Scriptures; or in which the reading of them has been greatly restrained. When this comparison is fairly made, I believe we shall find abundant cause to be thankful to the God and Father of all our mercies, for the benefit we enjoy, in having free access to those testimonials of his ways and will, respecting the children of men. Let them be fairly compared with the various systems of religion in the world; and then, although there should be some difficulties, which may not, at once, be fully comprehended, (and in what science are there not such difficulties?) then will the transcendent excellency of Christianity be felt and acknowledged; and gratitude fill the heart, for the unmerited love of God, in Christ Jesus our Lord.

Having fairly appreciated the general principles of Christianity, those which are peculiar to our religious society, and of which you make profession, will, I believe, rise in your view with esteem and attachment. Their consistency with the Christian religion has been already shown; and presuming you to be sensible of this consistency, I affectionately entreat you to be faithful in your adherence to them. Attend to that Divine Light, that saving grace, that good Spirit, which is placed in your hearts. This, if attended to, will preserve from the temptations incident to early life; and be your guide and support through the various trials and probations, which now, or hereafter, may be your allotment. O! my dear friends, receive this heavenly Visitant in the way of his coming. Give not up your minds to the pleasures and enjoyments of this world, which will draw away your obedient attention from things which make for true peace, and things by which you may edify one another. Be willing to take up the daily cross; and to bear the yoke of Him, who said : "Take my yoke upon you, and learn of me, for I am meek and lowly in heart, and ye shall find rest unto your souls; for my yoke is easy and my burden is light."*

Let those who have been habituated to sinful or dissipating pleasures, and have afterwards

* Matt. xi. 29, 30.

I

been brought to taste of the good word of life, and the powers of the world to come; let these say, whether more of the real comforts and enjoyments of life, are not to be experienced in the humility and self-denial of a Christian, than in all the gratifications which sin and folly afford.   When we take into consideration the divine peace, which we are told, "passeth all understanding;"* and a degree of which is at times the experience of the faithful followers of a crucified Lord; when we also consider the comfortable prospects of another and eternal state of existence, there will be found sufficient inducements, in every reasonable point of view, to prefer a life of religion and virtue, above that which is devoted to the indulgence and the pursuits of folly, dissipation, and sin.

The same principle of divine light, which led our predecessors out of the vain and sinful pleasures of the world, also let them see the corruptions which had taken place in religious worship and ministry; the inconsistency of war with the gospel dispensation; and the impropriety of divers other matters, in the external deportment of professing Christians.   For their testimony on these accounts, and the conduct consequent upon them, they suffered deeply, in an age when

* Phil. iv. 7.

religious liberty was claimed by all, but was given by few or none who came into the possession of power. Read the relations of the patient sufferings for the cause of truth, and the testimony of Jesus, of those who have gone before you;"* and faithfully bear your testimony even in those things that you may be ready to call little. Let not the singularity which a conduct consistent with your principles may produce, discourage you from a faithful adherence to them ; but submit to bear that cross, which will crucify you to the world, and the world to you, and redeem you from the various corruptions with which it abounds. The principles and practices of our society are now, in general, so respectfully treated, that the temptation to desert them is much lessened. Prize your privileges ; consider how differently our fore-fathers were circumstanced ; and let this consideration excite in your minds, increasing faithfulness and dedication to all parts of your religious duty. Follow the example of our blessed Redeemer ; remember the reproaches which he endured ;

---

* The Author wishes to turn the attention of the youth to the sufferings of the primitive Christians, and of the early reformers from popery, as well as to those of our own society.

and be willing to take up the cross and despise the shame; then you may become partakers of that crown of righteousness, which is the reward of all who have fonght the good fight, and kept the faith, and who love his appearance.

Before I conclude this address, I wish a little further to open the subject of Christian redemption, so far at least as to turn your attention to that work, which the depraved state of human nature renders universally necessary, and in which our Lord thus instructed a ruler among the Jews: " Except a man be born again, he cannot see the kingdom of God."* Whatever our religious profession, whatever our outward appearance and demeanour may be; all will fail to procure us Divine favour and acceptance, if the heart is not renewed after the image of Him that created us. " Marvel not that I said unto thee, ye must be born again."† This was the language in which our Saviour repeatedly inculcated this doctrine to Nicodemus; and oh! my dear young friends! neither marvel at it nor withdraw from it. Examine the state of your own hearts, and the occasion for it will soon be seen and felt. Dwell, therefore, I en-

* John iii. 3.   † John iii. 7.

treat you, under those divine convictions and influences, by which " the washing of regeneration and renewing of the Holy Ghost,"* are experienced. The work is generally slow and gradual ; therefore be not discouraged, if you cannot always perceive its progress: but as you abide patiently under a right exercise of mind, you will find that the work will in time proceed, until the new creation in Christ Jesus unto good works is known. But when this is in measure attained, still watchfulness and prayer should be the companions of every mind. The command to watchfulness is of universal extent: " What I say unto you, I say unto all, watch."† Again, " Watch and pray, that ye enter not into temptation."‡ When this disposition of mind is rightly abode in, it preserves from formality in religion ; keeps the soul alive to God ; and makes living members and bright examples in his church, and among his people. In this state of religious exercise, the experience of the primitive believers is attained : " By one spirit are we all baptized into one body ; and made to drink into one spirit."§ Here also right qualifications are received for religious service,

* Titus iii. 5.   † Mark xiii. 37.   ‡ Matt. xxvi. 41.
§ 1 Cor. xii. 13.

and a capacity to fill up the measure of suffering or labour, which may be allotted in the
church of Christ: a church, the members of
which are thus described by an inspired apostle:
"Ye also as lively stones are built up a spiritual
house, a holy priesthood, to offer up spiritual
sacrifices, acceptable to God by Jesus Christ."*

As one of the objects of this publication, is
to convey information to persons who are not
of our religious persuasion, I request that they
would follow the example of the noble Bereans,
and "search the scriptures whether those things
are so."+   It is not probable that we shall all
be brought to think alike on these subjects;
but if we can see, that so much may be said by
those from whom we differ, as to produce an
increase of Christian charity, something, and
something important, is gained.   I am not a fa-
vourer of that false charity, which would destroy
all religious zeal, and make all professions of
religion immaterial.   "Let every man be fully
persuaded in his own mind;"‡ and having endeavoured to obtain that persuasion from due
consideration, let him support it with zeal,
tempered with "the meekness of wisdom."

* 1 Peter ii. 5.   † Acts xvii. 11.   ‡ Rom. xiv. 5.

Thus, notwithstanding the variety of opinions into which the Christian world is divided, the light of the gospel will increase in the earth; and we may together promote the coming of that day, in which the divine promise and prediction will be fulfilled: "From the rising of the sun, even unto the going down of the same, my name shall be great among the Gentiles; and in every place, incense shall be offered unto my name, and a pure offering."* Then will "the kingdoms of this world, become the kingdoms of our Lord, and of his Christ; and he shall reign for ever and ever."†

* Mal. i. 11.   † Rev. xi. 15.

FINIS.

Printed by HARGROVE, GAWTHORP, and COBB, Herald-Office, Pavement, York.

LaVergne, TN USA
31 August 2009
156531LV00010B/157/A